Poets by Appointment

Britain's Laureates

For a Royal Wedding
29 July 1981

'Let's all in love and friendship hither come
Whilst the shrill Treble calls to thundering Tom,
And since the bells are for modest recreation
Let's rise and ring and fall to admiration.'

Those lines are taken from a ringer's rhyme
Composed in Cornwall in the Georgian time
From the high parish church of St. Endellion,
Loyal to the Monarch in the late Rebellion,
Loyal to King Charles the First and Charles the Second,
And through the Georges to our Prince of Wales,
A human, friendly line that never fails.
I'm glad that you are marrying at home
Below Sir Christopher's embracing dome;
Four square on that his golden cross and ball
Complete our own Cathedral of St. Paul.
Blackbirds in City churchyards hail the dawn,
Charles and Diana, on your wedding morn.
Come College youths, release your twelve-voiced power
Concealed within the graceful belfry tower
Till loud as breakers plunging up the shore
The land is drowned in one melodious roar.

A dozen years ago I wrote these lines:

'You knelt a boy, you rose a man
And thus your lonelier life began.'

The scene is changed, the outlook cleared,
The loneliness has disappeared.
And all of those assembled there
Are joyful in the love you share.

Poets by Appointment

Britain's Laureates

Nick Russel

BLANDFORD PRESS
POOLE DORSET

First published in the U.K. 1981 by
Blandford Press, Link House, West Street,
Poole, Dorset, BH15 1LL

British Library Cataloguing in Publication Data

Russell, Nick
Poets by appointment.
I. Title
821′.00941 PR505

ISBN 0 7137 1161 2

Filmset by August Filmsetting,
Reddish, Stockport.

Printed in Great Britain by Biddles Ltd, Guildford

Contents

		page
	Acknowledgments	vi
	Introduction	1
1	John Dryden (1631–1700)	9
2	Thomas Shadwell (1640?–1693)	20
3	Nahum Tate (1652–1715)	31
4	Nicholas Rowe (1674–1718)	43
5	Laurence Eusden (1688–1730)	55
6	Colley Cibber (1671–1757)	66
7	William Whitehead (1715–1785)	77
8	Thomas Warton (1728–1790)	89
9	Henry Pye (1745–1813)	101
10	Robert Southey (1774–1843)	113
11	William Wordsworth (1770–1850)	124
12	Alfred, Lord Tennyson (1809–1892)	133
13	Alfred Austin (1835–1913)	146
14	Robert Bridges (1844–1930)	159
15	John Masefield (1878–1967)	172
16	Cecil Day-Lewis (1904–1972)	184
17	John Betjeman (1906–)	193
	Index	200

Acknowledgments

The following have kindly given permission to reproduce copyright material: the *Daily Mail* for C. Day-Lewis's *Then and Now*; the *Evening Gazette*, Teesside, for C. Day-Lewis's *Hail Teesside!*; Sir John Betjeman for the *Jubilee Hymn* and the poem *For the Queen Mother*; John Murray (Publishers) Ltd for Sir John Betjeman's *4 November 1973*, which appears in his *Collected Poems*; *The Times* (1972, 1973, 1974, and 1977) for extracts from interviews with Sir John Betjeman; the Society of Authors as the literary representatives of the Estate of John Masefield. Poems by C. Day-Lewis on the investiture of Prince Charles (which first appeared in *The Guardian* in July 1969) and the *Battle of Britain* film *première* are reprinted by permission of A. D. Peters and Co. Ltd.

Two invaluable books on the laureates are Kenneth Hopkins *The Poets Laureate* (EP Publishing Ltd 1973) and E. K. Broadus *The Laureateship, a Study of the Office of Poet Laureate in England with some accounts of the Poets* (1921). Other useful sources have included Sean Day-Lewis *C. Day-Lewis: An English Literary Life* (Weidenfield 1980); Constance Babington Smith *John Masefield: A life* (OUP 1978); Montague Summers (ed.) *The Works of Thomas Shadwell* (1927); the Lord Chamberlain's Office; the Secretary for Appointments, 10 Downing Street; the British Library; the London Library; Trinity College Library, Cambridge; Cleveland County Library; Derek Coyte Ltd, London.

The 17th- and 18th- century poems used in this book come from a variety of printed sources, few of them definitive; where necessary, spelling and punctuation have been modified in order to achieve consistency of presentation and so make for easier reading. From Southey onward, however, no such difficulties exist as the poems can be found in most standard editions.

Introduction

Before Charles II's time a number of English kings had singled out the occasional contemporary poet for royal favours of one kind or another. In return, the recipient was expected to supply suitable verses praising the monarch's majesty, wisdom, or prowess. But until 1668, when Charles appointed John Dryden poet laureate—and used a warrant to do so—no sovereign had bothered to formalize the arrangement with a proper, official document.

The custom of crowning a poet with a wreath of bay, or sweet laurel, leaves originated in ancient Greece. By medieval times universities occasionally singled out a poet by calling him 'laureate', a term meaning distinguished, and so this academic usage came to be applied, more or less unofficially, to poets attached to the royal household.

Dryden's appointment, which made no mention of duties or remuneration, was not set out in any detail. That came two years later, when letters patent were issued confirming his status as poet laureate and also conferring on him the £200-a-year post of court historian, or historiographer royal. The patent stipulated the annual payment for the two posts together as £200, plus a butt (126 gallons) of 'the best Canary Wyne', the money being backdated to 1668, the date of the warrant.

Charles I, it is true, had started paying the poet and dramatist Ben Jonson a pension of 100 marks (£66⅔) in 1618, which had been increased to £100 and a quantity of Canary wine in 1630. But Jonson was being rewarded mainly for writing a series of elaborate masques for performance at court. His patents did not oblige him to perform any specific duties; he did not hold any office, nor did he call himself 'poet laureate'.

In 1638, more than a year after Jonson's death, William Davenant, who also wrote words for court masques, was likewise given a royal pension of £100. But his patent did not describe him as poet laureate, or mention Jonson, or contain any reference to verse-making or wine. Clearly, he was not succeeding to any established office involving the performance of specific duties. Four years later the civil war broke out, and the whole arrangement was allowed to lapse. In 1660, when Davenant (now knighted) returned from exile abroad, he found that Charles II was not prepared to renew the pension granted by his father.

Nevertheless, many people must have regarded Davenant as the king's officially appointed poet and so assumed that he had good claim to the title 'laureate'. When Davenant died in 1668, the antiquary John Aubrey wrote to a friend: 'Sir William was Poet Laureate, and Mr John Dryden hath his place.' It must have seemed a perfectly natural interpretation of events, although nobody could have known that this appointment marked the first stage in regularizing what was still a very tenuous relationship between monarch and aspiring poet. But the 1668 warrant covering Dryden's appointment refers specifically to 'a grant to John Dryden of the office of Poet Laureate, void by the death of Sir William Davenant'. It is this document that establishes Dryden unequivocally as the first man to hold the official title.

Charles chose Dryden because he was the best advocate available. But it was a long time before the laureate undertook work directly for the king. Instead, he devoted his time to his own affairs, supplying plays, poems, and essays that made him the leading professional writer of his day. By 1679, his total pension had risen to £300 a year, including £100 for the laureateship. In fact, Dryden wrote nothing official until the political crisis of 1681, when the earl of Shaftesbury tried to get the duke of Monmouth, a Protestant, made heir to the throne in place of Charles's brother James, a Roman Catholic. This led to Dryden's most famous poem, *Absalom and Achitophel*. But all the same, the idea for the satire itself had come from the king; and even *The Medal* (1682), a second attack on Shaftesbury, was apparently suggested by Charles. Dryden was equally loyal to James II, although the new king did stop the annual gift of wine. But in 1689 James was ousted by William III. Dryden, by now a Catholic, refused to swear allegiance, and was dismissed, the only time this has happened to a laureate.

The appointment of Thomas Shadwell to succeed Dryden was of course political—a Protestant Whig replacing a Catholic Tory. Shadwell's patent confirmed his salary at £300 (£100 as poet laureate, £200 as historiographer royal), and the butt of wine was generously restored. Three years later, however, when Nahum Tate became laureate, the king made a permanent change. The post of historiographer royal went elsewhere (it was finally abolished in 1860), leaving the laureate with £100 and the butt of Canary.

By the turn of the century it was becoming customary for odes in honour of the new year and the sovereign's birthday to be set to music and performed in St James's Palace. The Master of the King's Music wrote the music; but the odes were not yet an exclusive charge on the laureate—any poet could submit verses. Other important changes took place during Tate's laureateship. In 1702, when Anne came to the throne, the business of granting letters patent was streamlined, and Tate was reappointed with a simple certificate. In 1710 payment of the pension became a direct responsibility of the lord chamberlain's office, which put the laureate on the same footing as other servants of the royal household.

Nicholas Rowe, Tate's successor, was the first laureate to be appointed directly by the lord chamberlain. His arrival marks the beginning of a 100-year period of obligatory new year and birthday odes, a situation that lasted until the death of George III. As the century wore on, the job became little more than a routine. And if the salary was any clue to status, then the laureate counted for little—even the court barber could look forward to £170 a year.

With Laurence Eusden, at 30 the youngest man ever to become laureate, we reach a period of comparative stagnation. Eusden, who served from 1718 to 1730, is probably the least known of all the laureates; but then, unlike his predecessors, he never wrote a play or had any connection with the theatre. Almost mute if not completely inglorious, he was the first to have to tackle the problem of producing the same kind of official ode year after year.

As the office declined in importance, so did the significance of the laureate's political allegiance. Not that this bothered a man like Colley Cibber, Rowe's successor, who was far too successful a theatrical impressario to worry about other matters. But the £100 pension was certainly attractive to poorly paid writers. In 1730, for instance, the unsuccessful candidates included Stephen Duck, a Wiltshire farm worker, whose verses had won him the patronage of Queen Caroline; Lewis Theobald, poet, dramatist, and Shakespearean editor, the unenviable hero of Pope's *Dunciad* (1728); and Richard Savage, on whom the queen later settled £50 a year in return for an annual birthday ode. Until Cibber's time there was no procedure for publishing the laureate's official poems. But in 1731 the *Gentleman's Magazine* started to print the odes every year, which gave them considerable circulation.

Compulsory odes might have come to an end in 1757 when Cibber died. For the laureateship was offered to Thomas Gray—author of the *Elegy in a Country Churchyard* (1750)—on the understanding that biannual poems would no longer be required. The offer, which was, however, refused, arrived via William Mason, a close friend, to whom Gray sent a reply now famous for its observations on the office:

> Though I very well know the bland emollient saponaceous qualities both of sack and silver, yet if any great man would say to me, 'I make you rat-catcher to his Majesty, with a salary of £300 a year and two butts of the best Malaga; and though it has been usual to catch a mouse or two, for form's sake, in public once a year, yet to you, sir, we shall not stand upon these things,' I cannot say I should jump at it . . .

The arrival of William Whitehead, who succeeded Cibber, marked a new development. He realized that if the laureateship were to survive, its holder should be prepared to rise above the literary bickerings and political platitudes of the day, and concern himself with matters affecting the whole nation. But though he lived through events as stirring as the American Revolution, he seldom responded adequately to the challenges.

Thomas Warton, the next holder, came from the world of academic scholarship. Shortly before his appointment in 1785, he had become professor of ancient history at Oxford, having previously been professor of poetry there. He was mainly a literary historian, his *History of English Poetry* being a pioneer work in this field. During his term of office he was suddenly faced with a unique predicament. In November 1788 George III went mad only a few weeks before the new year ode was due. Tactfully, the laureate remained silent, and his luck held. George soon recovered, even going to St Paul's Cathedral for a service of thanksgiving in April 1789. When his birthday came round in June, Warton was able to refer to the king's misfortune obliquely, comparing it to storm clouds passing over the landscape.

On Warton's death in 1790 the laureateship was first offered to William Hayley, a famous poet of the time. The offer was made by William Pitt, the first prime minister to involve himself directly with the appointment. (It is now standard practice for the prime minister of the day to put forward names for the royal approval, and for the lord chamberlain, when commanded by the sovereign, to issue a warrant of appointment, which is for life. An announcement also appears in the *London Gazette*.) Hayley, however, had ample means, and refused; so Pitt gave the job to Henry James Pye, who had just lost his seat in the House of Commons. Once again, political considerations had won the day, for Pye was certainly no poet. In the roll-call of laureates he has only one claim to fame—he offered to forego the traditional gift of wine in exchange for cash. The government was only too pleased to agree; instead of paying out an extra £26 (the estimated value of the wine), they deemed this to be part of the basic £100. In 1810 George III became permanently insane, the Prince Regent took over, and birthday odes were no longer required.

In August 1813, a few days after Pye's death, Robert Southey, already well known as a poet, happened to be in London, and discovered that the Regent was prepared to bestow the post on him. Thanks to an administrative error, however, Walter Scott, then known only for his poetry, had also been approached—by the prime minister, Lord Liverpool. In the end Scott declined, putting forward the name of his friend Southey without of course knowing that that had been the Regent's original intention. Although Southey made valiant efforts to get the obligatory writing of odes abolished, he failed.

Southey ran into trouble with his very first new year ode, which had to be censored before it could be published. In January 1814

Napoleon's downfall seemed imminent, and the authorities argued that if a peace treaty were soon to restore friendly relations with France, it would not help to have condemned the French emperor as 'the perfidious Corsican' and worse.

When George IV became king in 1820 he had the good sense not to demand any more regular odes. Laureates were free to write only if the spirit moved them.

When Southey died in 1843 there was no doubt that his successor had to be the 73-year-old William Wordsworth. At first, he refused; but Sir Robert Peel, the prime minister, prevailed, explaining that the offer had not been made to impose onerous duties, 'but in order to pay you that tribute of respect which is justly due to the first of living poets'. Wordsworth is the oldest poet to have accepted the laureate's crown. Two years later, he travelled 300 miles from his home in the Lake district to Buckingham Palace. He wore court dress borrowed from the poet Samuel Rogers, seven years his senior, and carried a sword that had once belonged to his old friend Sir Humphry Davy, the chemist, who in 1800 had seen the second edition of *Lyrical Ballads* through the press. Although the dress was a tight fit, the poet managed to kneel at Queen Victoria's feet and kiss her hand.

Despite the promise of a laureateship free of duties, Wordsworth was asked to supply an ode for the inauguration of Prince Albert as Chancellor of Cambridge University in 1847. A poem was duly provided, but nobody knew that the real author was Edward Quillinan, Wordsworth's son-in-law. At the time, the old poet's favourite daughter was on her deathbed, and her father was in no mood for celebrations. He remains therefore the only laureate who never wrote a single poem connected with his office.

Alfred Tennyson, who followed Wordsworth in 1850, held office for a record 42 years. He was the first laureate to be on intimate terms with his sovereign, the only Englishman to be made a peer of the realm because he wrote poetry. But he was no automatic choice. Indeed, two days after Wordsworth's death in April, *The Times* was arguing for the office to end. Other interested parties wanted a woman to succeed, while Leigh Hunt, the essayist and poet, put forward his own name. Early in May, however, Prince

Albert wrote to Samuel Rogers, but he declined because he was now 87. Discussions continued into November, when Tennyson was at last approached. Evidently he was expecting something, for the night before the offer reached him, he dreamt Albert had kissed him on the cheek; whereupon he himself had observed, 'very kind, but very German'. Like his predecessor, the new laureate could not afford court dress; so he went to the palace wearing the outfit Wordsworth had borrowed.

Tennyson's death in 1892 produced a unique hiatus. Press speculation was considerable. The front runners included Algernon Swinburne, Rudyard Kipling, and William Morris. Finally, at the end of December 1895, Lord Salisbury, the new Conservative prime minister gave the job to Alfred Austin, Tory journalist, unsuccessful parliamentary candidate, and amateur poet. Twelve days later, Austin made an unexpected debut with a bombastic poem in praise of Dr Jameson's illegal invasion of the Boer republic of the Transvaal. It caused the government enormous embarrassment.

Since Austin's death in 1913, the laureateship has gone to men of a very different calibre. Robert Bridges, whom Herbert Asquith, the prime minister, chose in preference to such figures as Thomas Hardy and Laurence Binyon, was a dedicated poet of enormous technical ability. Like Tennyson, he was immensely respectable, and his collected poems had just launched him on a wave of unexpected popularity. During World War I he produced a number of poems about the conflict. But compared with the work of active-service poets such as Wilfred Owen and Isaac Rosenberg, his verses seem remote from the landscape of real warfare.

John Masefield, his successor, was the first laureate to be appointed by a Labour prime minister, Ramsay Macdonald. (Kipling was thought to be George V's first choice, A. E. Housman Macdonald's. But it was believed that each would refuse if approached.) Like Bridges, Masefield took his duties seriously, working hard to raise standards of verse speaking, and became the first president of the National Book League. He also started the practice, which his successors have followed, of chairing the committee that chooses the winner of the sovereign's Gold Medal for Poetry. Though prepared to tackle subjects as diverse as the launching of the *Queen*

Mary or the assassination of President John F. Kennedy, he was much associated with royal tributes. Early in World War II he broke new ground by writing a stirring account in prose of the evacuation of British and French forces from Dunkirk.

The appointment of Cecil Day-Lewis in 1968 marked a significant break with tradition, for he was a lifelong socialist and a former member of the Communist party, something that could not be said of any other laureate. In just over four years, he produced only a handful of official poems, but lent his valuable support to many activities in the field of art and literature.

When Day-Lewis died in 1972, there were many who hoped for a new type of laureate; if not a working-class poet, somebody who could at least speak for the poor. Sir John Betjeman, the present incumbent, hardly fits that description; yet as best-selling poet and TV personality he is familiar to millions. Over the years they have watched him describe the gloom and grandeur of Victorian architecture, or comment on the landscape of Britain as the ubiquitous camera swooped across its sunlit surface.

After more than three centuries of evolution, it seems unlikely that the laureateship will suddenly vanish overnight. Many social barriers are now down, and poetry, no longer the exclusive property of an élite, is a national asset. If there is real competition next time round, interest in the outcome should be enormous.

[1]
John Dryden
(1631–1700)

John Dryden's reputation has endured for nearly 300 years, but few people today read him much for pleasure. Nineteenth-century romantic writers still personify the archaetypal poet, whereas Dryden, who lived a fairly uneventful life, excelled in wit and satire, and earned his bread and butter writing for the stage, is not permitted in the same league.

The neglect is all the more regrettable, since his fellow writers have always recognized his abilities. Swinburne called him 'a sovereign orator', and T. S. Eliot praised his 'ability to make the small into the great, the prosaic into the poetic, the trivial into the magnificent'. But the greatest talent-spotter was Charles II. He could not have chosen a better man to lay the foundations of the laureateship.

When he became laureate in 1668 at the age of 37, Dryden was the first poet to be officially and unambiguously appointed to that post. To begin with he was paid nothing. But two years later letters patent were issued confirming him as laureate, and also appointing him historiographer royal (court historian), a post that carried a salary of £200. The patent laid down a payment of £200 a year for the combined position, together with a butt (about 126 gallons) of 'the best Canary Wyne'. The money was conveniently backdated to 1668. For the next few years the situation remained unchanged; but by 1679 there is documentary evidence that Dryden was enjoying an extra £100, specifically awarded for the laureateship. This is what Charles I had paid Sir William Davenant, his court poet, 'In consideration of services heretofore done and herefore to be done'. No doubt that arrangement, made before the civil war, was regarded in some way as a precedent.

Dryden, who was the eldest of 14 children, had been born in

August 1631 at Aldwinkle, Northamptonshire. He came from a Republican family that was zealously opposed to Charles. Indeed, his cousin Sir Gilbert Pickering was a close friend of Cromwell, and had been one of the judges at the king's trial (though not in court when the death sentence was passed). His first poem, an elegy on the death of a fellow pupil at Westminster School, was published when he was 18. But not until he was 29 did he produce anything to suggest he might one day be a major poet.

In 1654, when Dryden graduated from Trinity College, Cambridge, his father died, leaving him a farm. But the income was small, and by 1656 he had moved to London. There, thanks to Sir Gilbert, who was now lord chamberlain, he got a minor post. He was employed in the office of John Thurloe, responsible for foreign and home affairs as well as the secret service.

Dryden's early work as poet and playwright must have impressed Charles II. In 1658 he had mourned the death of Cromwell, in his *Heroic Stanzas*, which first established him as a poet. Two years later he rejoiced in the king's restoration, with his *Astrea Redux*. His enemies of course, never allowed him to forget his support for Cromwell; but if Dryden changed sides, so too did the rest of England. In 1661 he went on to celebrate Charles's coronation, and in 1662 he became one of the first fellows of the new Royal Society, which at once asked him to study ways of promoting the use of simple and lucid prose.

In 1667 appeared *Annus Mirabilis; the Year of Wonders*, Dryden's patriotic commemoration of the events of 1666, which he had written in the country, having left London to escape the plague. It included sea battles against the Dutch and a spectacular description of the Great Fire. In 1668 he brought out his most famous prose work, an essay on dramatic poetry, which discussed the art of writing and presenting plays for the stage.

But although Dryden became laureate in 1668, some 12 years were to pass before he wrote his first official poem. Then, in November 1681, apparently prompted by the king, he wrote his greatest poem, *Absalom and Achitophel*. Based on incidents in the Old Testament, this satire deals with the earl of Shaftesbury's attempt to debar the duke of York from the succession and to set the duke of

Monmouth, a bastard son of the king, in his place. The poem, which featured Charles as King David, was a runaway success.

Events now moved rapidly. In *The Medal* (1682) Dryden published another bitter attack on Shaftesbury, who had just been released from the Tower of London. Then the laureate himself came under fire, this time from an old opponent, Thomas Shadwell, dramatist and poet, who was eventually to succeed him. In a poem called *The Medal of John Bayes* (a nickname fastened on Dryden ten years before) Shadwell wrote up every tale he knew about the laureate. Dryden replied with *Mac Flecknoe*, a short personal attack, which appeared late in 1682 and virtually flattened Shadwell. The poem, a favourite of the author's, pillories Shadwell as the dullest writer of his day. Dryden completed the demolition later that year with a second part of *Absalom and Achitophel*. Although this was composed largely by Nahum Tate (poet laureate after Shadwell), it was revised by Dryden, who himself contributed some 200 lines of telling invective. These included a memorable word-picture of a drunken, fat Shadwell rolling home from a 'treason-tavern':

> A monstrous mass of foul corrupted matter,
> As all the devils had spewed to make the batter.

The rest of Dryden's official output did not amount to much. His *Religio Laici* (a layman's religion) published in that busy year of 1682, was not apparently written to order. But his defence of the Anglican Church must have pleased many—though few could have supposed its author would soon change his faith and bring out an equally sincere defence (*The Hind and the Panther*, 1687) of the papacy. The unfortunate timing of Dryden's conversion—early in 1686—upset many people, then and now. But despite the force of Dr Samuel Johnson's observation, 'That conversion will always be suspected that apparently concurs with interest', Dryden seems to have been absolutely sincere. He certainly made sure his three sons were brought up as Catholics.

When Charles had a stroke and died in February 1685, Dryden saluted his memory with *Threnodia Augustalis*, now worth recalling only for the lively description of the doctors milling around the royal deathbed:

The extremest ways they first ordain,
Prescribing such intolerable pain,
As none but Caesar could sustain:
Undaunted Caesar underwent
The malice of their art, nor bent
Beneath whate'er their pious vigour could invent:
In five such days he suffered more
Then any suffered in his reign before;

The atmosphere of surprising calm in which King James II, an avowed Roman Catholic, took over from his brother must have reassured most Catholics, especially recent converts like Dryden. Admittedly, there was always the problem of what might happen when James died and the Protestant succession was inevitably resumed. But for the time being all was well. Indeed, in June 1688 the king's wife Mary, after 14 childless years, unexpectedly gave birth to a son, James Edward Stuart. Rejoicing among Catholics was of course widespread, because if the baby survived, the succession would be Catholic. *Britannia Rediviva*, Dryden's last official poem, as it happened, was quickly written to celebrate the birth of the new prince. But James II had antagonized too many of his subjects by his over-vigorous promotion of Catholics to positions of power and influence. Within 18 months, William of Orange had landed in England, to become William III, and both James and his laureate (and historiographer) were dispossessed. Dryden's place went to Shadwell, and the baby he had hailed as 'so great a blessing to so good a king' passed into history as the Old Pretender.

For the remaining 12 years of his life, Dryden was compelled to work very hard, even returning for a while to writing for the stage. His comedy, *Amphitryon* (1690), with music by Henry Purcell, turned out to be one of his greatest successes, and encouraged him to refurbish his opera, *King Arthur*, first produced in 1685. The music for the new version was also by Purcell.

Despite this work for the theatre, Dryden put his main effort into translations, the most successful being his complete Virgil, which came out in 1697. It was done, he said, 'in my declining years; struggling with wants, oppress'd with sickness, curb'd in my genius, liable to be misconstrued in all I write'. His final great work was *The Fables* (1700), a translation of stories by Chaucer, Boccaccio, and Ovid, written, despite his age, with tremendous vigour. Appropriately enough, his last job was for the theatre, supplying a masque to follow a play. The closing lines

'Tis well an old age is out,
And time to begin a new.

were the very last words he wrote. He died in London on May Day 1700, having steadily refused to have a toe amputated to prevent gangrene spreading to the rest of his body. On 12 May he was buried with great ceremony in Poet's Corner, Westminster Abbey, between Abraham Cowley (the 'darling of his youth') and Chaucer ('here is God's plenty').

Absalom and Achitophel

Absalom and Achitophel *was written to set public opinion against the earl of Shaftesbury and the Whigs, and appeared on 17 November 1681, a week before the grand jury threw out the bill against Shaftesbury on a charge of high treason. The characters in these opening lines—which make up nearly a quarter of the whole poem—include David (Charles II), Absalom (duke of Monmouth), Achitophel (Shaftesbury), Michal (Catherine of Braganza, the king's childless wife), Annabel (Monmouth's wife), Saul and Ishbosheth (Cromwell and his son Richard). The Jews represent the English, the Jebusites the Roman Catholics, and the Egyptians the French.'that Plot' (p. 16) refers to the alleged Popish Plot to kill the king and hand over government to the Jesuits.*

In pious times, ere priestcraft did begin,
Before polygamy was made a sin;
When man, on many, multiply'd his kind,
Ere one to one was, cursedly, confind:
When Nature prompted, and no law deny'd
Promiscuous use of concubine and bride;
Then, Israel's monarch, after Heaven's own heart,
His vigorous warmth did, variously, impart

To wives and slaves: and, wide as his command,
Scatter'd his Maker's image through the land.
Michal, of royal blood, the crown did wear,
A soil ungrateful to the tiller's care:
Not so the rest; for several mothers bore
To godlike David, several sons before.
But since like slaves his bed they did ascend,
No true succession could their seed attend.
Of all this numerous progeny was none
So beautiful, so brave as Absalon:
Whether, inspir'd by some diviner lust,
His father got him with a greater gust;
Or that his conscious destiny made way
By manly beauty to imperial sway.
Early in foreign fields he won renown,
With kings and states ally'd to Israel's crown:
In peace the thoughts of war he could remove,
And seem'd as he were only born for love.
Whate'er he did was done with so much ease,
In him alone, 'twas natural to please.
His motions all accompanied with grace;
And Paradise was open'd in his face.
With secret joy, indulgent David view'd
His youthful image in his son renew'd:
To all his wishes nothing he deny'd,
And made the charming Annabel his bride.
What faults he had (for who from faults is free?)
His father could not, or he would not see.
Some warm excesses, which the law forbore,
Were constru'd youth that purg'd by boiling o'er,
And Amnon's murder, by a specious name,
Was call'd a just revenge for injur'd fame.
Thus prais'd and lov'd, the noble youth remained,
While David, undisturb'd, in Sion reign'd.
But life can never be sincerely blest:
Heaven punishes the bad, and proves the best.
The Jews, a headstrong, moody, murmuring race,

As ever tried the extent and stretch of grace;
God's pamper'd people whom, debauch'd with ease,
No king could govern, nor no God could please;
(Gods they had tried of every shape and size,
That god-smiths could produce, or priests devise:)
These Adam-wits, too fortunately free,
Began to dream they wanted liberty;
And when no rule, no precedent was found
Of men, by laws less circumscrib'd and bound
They led their wild desires to woods and caves,
And thought that all but savages were slaves.
They who when Saul was dead, without a blow,
Made foolish Ishbosheth the crown forego;
Who banisht David did from Hebron bring,
And with a general shout proclaim'd him king:
Those very Jews, who, at their very best,
Their humour more than loyalty exprest,
Now wonder'd why so long they had obey'd
An idol monarch, which their hands had made;
Thought they might ruin him they could create;
Or melt him to that golden calf, a state.
But these were random bolts: no form'd design,
Nor interest made the factious crowd to join:
The sober part of Israel, free from stain,
Well knew the value of a peaceful reign;
And, looking backward with a wise affright,
Saw seams of wounds dishonest to the sight:
In contemplation of whose ugly scars,
They curst the memory of civil wars.
The moderate sort of men, thus qualif'd,
Inclin'd the balance to the better side:
And David's mildness manag'd it so well,
The bad found no occasion to rebel.
But, when to sin our biassed Nature leans,
The careful Devil is still at hand with means;
And providently pimps for ill desires:
The good old cause reviv'd, a Plot requires.

Plots, true or false, are necessary things,
To raise up commonwealths, and ruin kings.

Th' inhabitants of old Jerusalem
Were Jebusites: the town so call'd from them;
And their's the native right—
But when the chosen people grew more strong,
The rightful cause became the wrong:
And every loss the men of Jebus bore,
They still were thought God's enemies the more.
Thus, worn and weaken'd, well or ill content,
Submit they must to David's government:
Impoverisht, and depriv'd of all command,
Their taxes doubled as they lost their land,
And, what was harder yet to flesh and blood,
Their Gods disgrac'd, and burnt like common wood.
This set the heathen priesthood in a flame;
For priests of all religions are the same:
Of whatsoe'r descent their godhead be,
Stock, stone, or other homely pedigree,
In his defence his servants are as bold
As if he had been born of beaten gold.
The Jewish rabbins, tho' their enemies,
In this conclude them honest men and wise:
For 'twas their duty, all the learned think,
T'espouse his cause by whom they eat and drink.
From hence began that Plot, the nation's curse,
Bad in itself, but represented worse:
Rais'd in extremes, and in extremes decry'd;
With oaths affirm'd, with dying vows deny'd:
Not weigh'd, or winnow'd by the multitude;
But swallow'd in the mass, unchew'd and crude.
Some truth there was, but dash'd and brew'd with lies;
To please the fools, and puzzle all the wise.
Succeeding times did equal folly call,
Believing nothing, or believing all.
Th' Egyptian rites the Jebusites imbrac'd;

Where gods were recommended by their taste.
Such savory deities must needs be good,
As serv'd at once for worship and for food.
By force they could not introduce these gods;
For ten to one, in former days was odds.
So fraud was used (the sacrificer's trade)
Fools are more hard to conquer than persuade.
Their busy teachers mingled with the Jews;
And rak'd, for converts, even the court and stews:
Which Hebrew priests the more unkindly took,
Because the fleece accompanies the flock.
Some thought they God's Anointed meant to slay
By guns, invented since full many a day:
Our author swears it not; but who can know
How far the Devil and Jebusites may go?
This Plot, which fail'd for want of common sense,
Had yet a deep and dangerous consequence:
For, as when raging fevers boil the blood,
The standing lake soon floats into a flood;
And every hostile humour, which before
Slept quiet in its channels, bubbles o'er:
So, several factions from this first ferment,
Work up to foam, and threat the government.
Some by their friends, more by themselves thought wise,
Oppos'd the power, to which they could not rise.
Some had in courts been great, and thrown from thence,
Like fiends, were harden'd in impenitence.
Some, by their monarch's fatal mercy grown,
From pardon'd rebels, kinsmen to the throne,
Were rais'd in power and public office high:
Strong bands, if bands ungrateful men could tie.
Of these the false Achitophel was first:
A name to all succeeding ages curst:
For close designs, and crooked counsels fit;
Sagacious, bold, and turbulent of wit:
Restless, unfixt in principles and place;
In power unpleas'd, impatient of disgrace:

A fiery soul, which working out its way,
Fretted the pigmy body to decay:
And o'er-inform'd the tenement of clay,
A daring pilot in extremity;
Pleas'd with the danger, when the waves went high
He sought the storms; but for a calm unfit,
Would steer too near the sands, to boast his wit.
Great wits are sure to madness near ally'd;
And thin partitions do their bounds divide:
Else, why should he, with wealth and honour blest,
Refuse his age the needful hours of rest?
Punish a body which he could not please;
Bankrupt of life, yet prodigal of ease?
And all to leave, what with his toil he won,
To that unfeather'd, two leg'd thing, a son:
Got, while his soul did huddled notions try;
And born a shapeless lump, like anarchy.
In friendship false, implacable in hate:
Resolv'd to ruin or to rule the state.
To compass this the triple bond he broke;
The pillars of the public safety shook:
And fitted Israel for a foreign yoke.
Then seiz'd with fear, yet still affecting fame,
Usurp'd a patriot's all-atoning name.
So easy still it proves in factious times,
With public zeal to cancel private crimes:
How safe is treason, and how sacred ill,
Where none can sin against the people's will:
Where crowds can wink; and no offence be known,
Since in another's guilt they find their own.
Yet, fame deserv'd, no enemy can grudge;
The statesman we abhor, but praise the judge.
In Israel's courts ne'er sat an Abbethdin
With more discerning eyes, or hands more clean:
Unbrib'd, unsought, the wretched to redress;
Swift of dispatch, and easy of access.
Oh, had he been content to serve the crown,

With virtues only proper to the gown;
Or, had the rankness of the soil been freed
From cockle, that opprest the noble seed:
David, for him his tuneful harp had strung,
And Heaven had wanted one immortal song.
But wild Ambition loves to slide, not stand;
And Fortune's ice prefers to Virtue's land:
Achitophel, grown weary to possess
A lawful fame, and lazy happiness:
Disdain'd the golden fruit to gather free,
And lent the crowd his arm to shake the tree.
Now, manifest of crimes, contriv'd long since,
He stood at bold defiance with his prince:
Held up the buckler of the people's cause,
Against the crown; and sculk'd behind the laws.
The wish'd occasion of the Plot he takes,
Some circumstances finds, but more he makes;
By buzzing emissaries, fills the ears
Of listning crowds, with jealousies and fears
Of arbitrary counsels brought to light,
And proves the king himself a Jebusite:
Weak arguments! which yet he knew full well,
Were strong with people easy to rebel.
For, govern'd by the moon, the giddy Jews
Tread the same track when she the prime renews:
And once in twenty years, their scribes record,
By natural instinct they change their lord.
Achitophel still wants a chief, and none
Was found so fit as warlike Absalon:
Not, that he wish'd his greatness to create,
(For politicians neither love nor hate:)
But, for he knew, his title not allow'd,
Would keep him still depending on the crowd:
That kingly power, thus ebbing out, might be
Drawn to the dregs of a democracy.
Him he attempts, with studied arts to please,
And sheds his venom, in such words as these . . .

[2]

Thomas Shadwell

(1640?–1693)

Thomas Shadwell has had a bad press for 300 years. Ever since he had the misfortune to be ridiculed by Dryden, the great master of invective, few authorities on the period have bothered to take an impartial look at the surviving evidence, most of it derived from hostile witnesses. But once we recognize the extent to which prejudice and snobbery have intervened—unfortunately Shadwell was *only* a skilful and successful dramatist—the caricature begins to fade, giving us a much better chance of discovering what he was really like.

He was born in Norfolk, sometime between 1640 and 1642, either at Broomhill House, a few miles from Thetford, or at nearby Santon House, both of which were properties belonging to his father, John Shadwell, a successful lawyer. Thomas, who was one of 11 children, spent a year at the grammar school in Bury St Edmunds, Suffolk, before entering Caius College, Cambridge, in December 1656. After leaving university, he went to read law at the Middle Temple in London; but he soon gave that up in favour of the theatre, which was then enjoying a new lease of life.

In 1642, when the civil war began, the Puritan authorities had closed the theatres, which stayed shut until the return of Charles II in 1660. But the king, anxious to control the stage, limited the number of companies to two, sometimes one. Unlike their predecessors, the new playhouses were roofed in and used oil lamps for lighting; acting took place on a 'picture-frame' stage, with a platform projecting into the audience; and for the first time women played the feminine roles. The plays themselves were either heroic tragedies, about love and honour, usually in rhymed couplets; or sophisticated comedies, often coarse and immoral.

Shadwell's first play was a comedy, *The Sullen Lovers, or the*

Impertinents, produced in May 1668. It was based on a work by the French dramatist Molière (1622–73), and Shadwell's wife, an actress called Anne Gibbs, played the heroine. The diarist Samuel Pepys, who saw the opening performance, found 'many good humours in it, but the play tedious, and no design at all in it'. However, it proved a great success, and for the next 13 years hardly a season went by without some new Shadwell play.

Pepys's reference to humours shows that he recognized the influence of the Elizabethan dramatist Ben Jonson, who was Shadwell's great hero. Each character in a typical Jonson play personifies a particular quality, or humour, the production being designed to portray such qualities in action. Shadwell's preface to *The Sullen Lovers* fully acknowledged the debt to Jonson, 'the man of all the world I most passionately admire for his excellency in dramatic poetry . . .' But, unfortunately, his remarks brought him into conflict with John Dryden, who had just become poet laureate. Shadwell accused him of underestimating Jonson's comic genius. Although the accusation went unanswered (indeed, the two men remained friends for some time), it proved to be the first skirmish in a long feud.

Within two or three years of starting, Shadwell had become known as a gifted dramatist—his friend John Aubrey, the antiquarian, called him 'the best comedian we have now'. His fourth play, *The Miser* (1671?), again based on a recent comedy by Molière, was dedicated to the earl of Dorset, his first patron. His other benefactors included the elderly duke of Newcastle, who had been Jonson's patron before the civil war; to him Shadwell dedicated *Epsom Wells* (1672), one of his most popular pieces.

In 1673 Shadwell struck out in a new direction—an operatic adaptation of Shakespeare's *Tempest*. The staging was elaborate; and, for the first time, it seems, the musicians sat in front of the stage, not on it or behind the scenery. Perhaps Shadwell was deliberately measuring himself against Dryden, who had produced his own version of the same play in 1667, in collaboration with Sir William Davenant. (Davenant, who died in 1668, was a great theatrical innovator. During the Commonwealth, he had been the only man allowed to stage theatrical performances, though these were really musical entertainments, which he described in neutral terms as 'operas'.) Shadwell's second operatic work, *Psyche*, adapted from an opera by the French composer Lully, appeared the following year. Written in rhymed verse, it was lavishly staged—production costs came to £800—and included a ballet. The music was by Matthew Locke, one of the founders of English opera, who had worked with Shadwell on his *Tempest*.

In 1676 Shadwell produced *The Libertine*, a tragedy featuring Don Juan as the hero. Incidental music and songs, which included the still popular 'Nymphs and shepherds', were by Henry Purcell, soon to become the most distinguished musician of his time. Later that year came *The Virtuoso*, a delightful send-up of the bizarre activities pursued by members of the Royal Society (founded 1660). Its most engaging character is Sir Nicholas Gimcrack, a connoisseur of air, who collects samples from different parts of the country for his guests to savour.

In 1678 England was shaken by the Popish Plot, an imaginary conspiracy 'discovered' by two clergymen, Titus Oates and Israel Tonge. Oates claimed that the Roman Catholics were planning to kill the king, put his Catholic brother James on the throne, and burn London. Popular feeling was so intense, James was forced into temporary exile, and the earl of Shaftesbury, who led the opposition to Charles II, became the most influential politician in the country.

The general election of February 1679 was the first fought more or less on party lines. Shaftesbury's Country Party, the Whigs, decisively defeated the Court Party, who had become identified with the Catholic cause and were known as Tories. The Whigs now tried to exclude James from the succession and have the duke of Monmouth, Charles's eldest son, made heir to the throne. But Monmouth was indisputably a bastard, and his father refused to negotiate. Finally, in March 1681, Charles dissolved Parliament, and the opposition rapidly collapsed. Although Shaftesbury was arrested in July and charged with treason, he was acquitted four months later. But he failed to rally the country against the king. In November 1682 he fled to Holland, where he soon died.

The Whig rejoicing at Shaftesbury's release in December 1681 was shortlived. Instead, all London revelled in Dryden's newly published satirical poem, *Absalom and Achitophel*, which featured Monmouth as King David's favourite son and Shaftesbury as his wily adviser. The king himself was thought to have commissioned the work. As the tide turned in favour of the Tories, Dryden, prompted (it was again said) by the king, delivered his second broadside, *The Medal*—so-called because Shaftesbury's supporters had had a medal struck to celebrate his release from the Tower, where he had been imprisoned.

Of course, the Whigs were not to be outdone. In May 1682, eight weeks after *The Medal* appeared, Shadwell produced his counterblast, *The Medal of John Bayes*. Describing Dryden (Bayes) as 'a cherry-cheeked dunce of fifty-three', he did everything he could to smear the laureate. Dryden's *Mac Flecknoe*, first printed in 1682 in a pirated edition, returned the compliment with interest. Written with heavy sexual innuendo, it describes how Shadwell ascends the throne of Dulness to become monarch of Non-sense, an idea that gave Pope the starting point for his *Dunciad* (1728). Six weeks later came Dryden's final onslaught, a second part of *Absalom and Achitophel*. Most of it was written by Nahum Tate, Shadwell's successor as poet laureate, but the sustained caricature of Shadwell was by Dryden.

Unlike Dryden, however, the unfortunate Shadwell was not prepared to trim politically when things were bad. As a result, no further play of his was performed until *The Squire of Alesia*, a comedy about low life in London, was staged in May 1688.

With the accession of William III (February 1689), Dryden was dismissed from office, and Shadwell became poet laureate. No doubt, he found it a fitting reward for his years of loyalty to the Whig cause. During his three and a half years of office, he seems to have written no more than half a dozen set pieces. But perhaps his most significant contribution was *Votum Perenne, A Poem to the King on New Year's Day* (1690), which helped to set the fashion for producing an ode each 1 January, an event that soon became a regular feature of the literary scene.

Shadwell died on 19 November 1693 from an overdose of opium, which he had taken for years to relieve the gout. *The*

Gentleman's Journal, a monthly periodical, was quick to pay its tribute:

> All those that love to see the image of human nature, lively drawn in all the various colours and shapes with which it is diversified in our age, must own that few living have equalled that admirable master in his draughts of humours and characters.

We have no way of knowing what Dryden thought of that. But Shadwell himself would have liked it, especially the reference to humours.

For Queen Mary's Birthday 1691

Queen Mary II, daughter of the Roman Catholic James II, was a staunch Protestant and strong supporter of the Church of England. She was only 15 when married to William of Orange, who was 27, in 1677. She and William did not reign by hereditary right (that remained with James), but were declared joint-sovereigns. William was in fact England's first constitutional monarch. Parliament decided that James had 'abdicated'—which was untrue. Henceforth the crown lost the power, previously enjoyed by James, of suspending or dispensing with the laws and could no longer maintain a standing army in peacetime. Mary had no children and died of smallpox on 28 December 1694.

  Welcome, welcome, glorious Morn,
  Nature smiles at thy return.
At thy return the joyful earth
Renews the blessings of *Maria's* birth.
The busy sun prolongs his race
The youthful year his earliest tribute pays
And frosts forsake his head and tears his face.
  Welcome, welcome, glorious Morn,
  Nature smiles at thy return,
For Nature's richest pride with thee was born.

Welcome as when three happy kingdoms strove
In glad confusion to express their love,
When ev'ry heart did ev'ry tongue employ
To speak its share of public joy,
And great *Maria's* birth proclaim
The noblest theme, the loudest song of fame.

The mighty Goddess of this wealthy isle
Rais'd her glad head, and with an awful smile
She look'd, whilst thousand cupids hover'd round
And thousand graces the fair infant crown'd.
  Full of wonder and delight
  She saw and bless'd the noble sight.
And lo! a sacred fury swell'd her breast,
And the whole God her lab'ring soul possest.
To lofty strains her tuneful lyre she strung
And thus the Goddess play'd and thus she sung.

My pray'rs are heard, Heav'n has at last bestow'd
The mighty blessings which it long has ow'd,
At length the bounteous gods have sent us down
A brightness second only to their own.
  I see the round years successively move
  To ripen her beauties and crown 'em with love;
  A hero renown'd in virtues and arms
  Shall wear the soft chain and submit to her charms,
  And *Hymen* and *Hebe* shall make it their care
  To pour all their joys on the valiant and fair.
  Then, then, our sad *Albion* shall suffer no more,
  She shall fly to his aid and be freed by his pow'r,
  And date all her blessings from this happy hour.

He to the field by honour call'd shall go
And dangers he shall know and wonders he shall do.
The God of arms his godlike son shall bless
And crown his fleet and armies with success.
Whilst undisturb'd his happy consort reigns

And wisely rules the kingdoms he maintains.
Britain at last shall see her peace restor'd
And pay new vows for her returning lord:
Maria then shall all her cares unbend
And she shall still adorn and he defend.

Sound, all ye spheres; confirm the omen, Heav'n,
And long preserve the blessings thou hast giv'n.

On His Majesty's Conquests in Ireland 1692

William III was the focus of European opposition to Louis XIV. His accession to the throne in 1689 inaugurated a period of war with France that was to last into the 19th century. Britain could win this conflict only by asserting its naval supremacy, and this it was quick to do with regard to Ireland, where resistance by the forces of James II depended entirely on the maintenance of communications with France. But on 19 May 1692 the crushing defeat of the French fleet near Cape La Hogue, off the Normandy peninsula, ended all fears of invasion. Shadwell, aware of the strategic implications, therefore seized the opportunity to recall William III's successes in Ireland, which had begun on 1 July 1690 with the battle of the Boyne, where James II was decisively beaten. (This is the battle still celebrated today by Protestants in Northern Ireland.) Marshal Friedrich Schomberg, an elderly soldier of fortune, commanded the English expedition in Ireland.

How great a transport is a brave man in,
When echoing trumpets bid the fight begin?
With joy, the list'ning warrior hears them sound,
And rears himself, all ravish'd, from the ground:
He grasps his sword, and lifts his pond'rous shield,
And big with joy, flies to the fatal field:
The God of War his heated breast inspires,
And his glad soul swells to receive the fires:

Already, he descries the distant plain,
Already seems to view the horrid scene,
Hear clashing spears, and groans of dying men.
Such was our monarch's transport at the Boyne:
There, Nassau, all the work was Heaven's, and thine.
Thyself the foremost, like the leading god,
Thy soldiers gladly follow'd thro' the flood;
Bending the waves beneath them with their tread,
They rais'd a tempest, tho' the winds were laid.
Each army, like a well-appointed fleet,
Cut thro' the rapid streams, and midway met;
Whilst from both shores the thund'ring ordnance speaks,
In louder sounds, than those of brazen beaks.
All elements, fire, water, earth and air,
Join in the fight, and mingle in the war.
Clouds of black smoke the face of Heav'n obscure,
The earth is shook, and the dash'd waters roar;
Hundreds are swallowed up, the furious tide,
With a strong current, rowls away the dead.
Already they have shot the gulf of death,
And need no wastage over lakes beneath;
Fate stretch'd himself, and both the banks bestride,
Fixing a deadly foot on either side,
Whilst underneath his arch the river flow'd,
Whose waters rose up to him, swell'd with blood;
By thousand differing ways, a thousand fall,
See death in all its forms, and dire in all.
The stately youth, that stood erect but now,
Struck by the mortal dart, are levelled low;
Whole heads and arms are lopt, the shivering spear
Strikes its sharp splinters thro' the wounded air;
All instruments of death the fates employ,
Whom the swords spare, the waters do destroy.
From dying chiefs the river gains a fame,
But Schomberg gives it an immortal name:
Bred up in camps, inur'd to horrid wars,
Loaden with fame and honour, as with years;

Brave as he liv'd, the good old general fell,
And his great master did revenge him well.
O! had thy mighty shade been by t' have seen
What troops of ghosts he sent to wait on thine,
Thy thankful *Genius* would his steps attend,
The best of masters, and the bravest friend;
To him thy art of conquering would bequeath,
Who fought to make thee famous in thy death:
For whilst the waters of the Boyne shall flow,
Succeeding ages shall remember you.

Soldiers and chiefs without distinction drop,
Only the king, stood as immortal up;
Around thy head a thousand deaths did fly,
Spent in the air; the boldest destiny
Durst only touch thee in its passage by.
Thy stronger *Genius* did the stroke decline,
Fate had the power of ev'ry life but thine.
Heroes on either side rush dauntless on;
The day is vanish'd ere the battle's done.
Groans of fall'n soldiers mount up to the skies,
Compassionate Echo's answer to their cries.
Whole Heav'ns concern'd, as 'twere itself in fight,
And diseased Nature sickens at the sight;
Nought stops the merc'less victor in his course,
Strongly he urges on th' impetuous horse,
And bears down all with a resistless force:
So swiftly does he drive the flying steed,
That victory can scarce keep equal speed.
Heaven looks with pity on the mighty dead,
And griev'd to see so many thousands bleed,
Spreads the thick veil of night, to keep them hid.
The sun went down with an unwonted red;
Bloody he lookt, as if himself had bled.
He seem'd to fall in the same famous stream;
Our Nassau fought, and seem'd to fall by him.
Those very waters where the god lay drown'd,

Our greater hero past and went beyond.
The heavens withdraw their lustre, and their fires
And day itself, the last of all, expires.
Night, horror, and confusion, fill the plain,
Darkness and death, shut in the gloomy scene.

Winds waft the dreadful tidings round their coast;
Aloud they tell them how their isle is lost;
Bid them take wings, and fly in haste away,
The conqeror comes on, as swift as they.
Fierce, and resistless, through the land he past;
His fame, and he seem'd to make equal haste.
At his approach th'affrighted realm is shook,
The chiefest cities yield without a stroke.
To the proud walls of Limrick, siege he lays,
Which nought but winter had the power to raise.
The gathering clouds do warn him to be gone,
And timely shew the tempest drawing on.
His orders for a brave retreat are given,
The pious hero only yields to Heaven.
So Tyre stopt Alexander's eager haste;
Withstood him for a while, tho' won at last.
Now he returns from the half-vanquished isle;
And seeks in foreign camps for nobler toil.
He leaves his army to his general's care,
And shews the ways, they must pursue the war.
With the vast help of the dread Nassau's name,
His gallant chiefs purchase their share of fame.
They fought secure of honour, and success;
The cause was Heavens, and the army his.
Conquest is easier made, when once begun;
Like high swoln waters, when the sluice is drawn,
The torrent from afar comes rowling on.

To distant realms his conquering arms he bears,
And hostile lands are made the seat of wars.
On him, and us these blessings are bestow'd,

Peace flourishes at home, and war abroad.
Disdainful princes are compell'd to bow;
And haughty France begins to feel us now.
With powers unequal, they a war maintain,
Compelled already to resign the main.
The greatest navy they could ever boast,
The work of thirty years, one conflict lost.
Both fleets encountred with impetuous shocks,
Resounding as the waves, that dash the rocks.
The cannon roar'd as loud as did the seas,
And fire, and smoke rowl'd o'er the ocean's face,
Some sunk, some scatter'd through the wat'ry field,
And some from farther flight disabl'd yield.
Once more, we're sovereign masters of the sea,
And have our passage to invasion free.
On the proud foe, we may our armies pour,
Resistless as the seas, that wash their shore.
Again, we may recover empire there:
England can do it, and its monarch dare.
'Tis he must pull the growing tyrant down;
'Tis he will lead the British armies on.
Go all you gallant youths, your arms prepare,
Go with your royal leader to the war.
Yours is the right, with conquest make your claim,
And raise at once, your fortunes and your fame.
None but old men confin'd within our isles,
And tender maids, unfit for mighty toils.
Albion unpeopled, need not fear surprise,
Heaven has created it a guard of seas.
The aged sires to altars shall repair,
And with a pious force, win heaven by prayer.
The sighing virgins shall your absence mourn,
And every beauty beg your safe return
With vows and tears, assenting heaven shall move,
And that shall crown your arms, and they your love.

[3]
Nahum Tate
(1652–1715)

Today the name of Nahum Tate is all but forgotten—except in learned footnotes. Yet every winter, when grown-ups sing or children parody the Christmas hymn 'While shepherds watched their flocks by night', he lives again. For this was one of the most popular pieces in the *New Version of the Psalms of David* (1696), which he compiled with the Rev. Nicholas Brady. (The hymn itself first appeared in 1700, in a supplement). Tate was also the first poet to sing the praises of our national drink, in a poem called *Panacea, a Poem upon Tea.*

As laureate he achieved little success; but this 'honest, quiet man with downcast face and somewhat given to "fuddling"', as William Oldys, a near-contemporary, described him, had quite a lot to be proud of.

Born in Dublin in 1652, the son of Faithful Teate, an Irish clergyman, Nahum Tate was named after the Old Testament prophet who predicted the destruction of Nineveh. He was educated at Trinity College, Dublin. He graduated in 1672; but instead of entering the church, he went to London to seek his fortune.

Within a few years he had written enough verse to justify publishing a collection of poems, which appeared in 1677. But the theatre was where he was destined to make his name, and his first play, *Brutus of Alba, or the Enchanted Lovers*, a tragedy, was presented the following year. Founded on the story of Dido, queen of Carthage, the play was dedicated to Thomas Shadwell's patron, the earl of Dorset.

Tate's next play, *The Loyal General* (1680), was graced with a prologue by John Dryden, the poet laureate. But it was with *The Sicilian Usurper* (1681), an adaptation of Shakespeare's *Richard II*, that he discovered the advantages of plundering the works of past writers. He so altered the text that every scene was, as he put it, 'full of respect to Majesty and the dignity of Courts'. Charles II decided that the political parallels were far too explicit, however, and *The Sicilian Usurper* was taken off after three days. Later that year Tate produced what was to be, far and away, his most successful adaptation—the famous revision of *King Lear*, Shakespeare's greatest tragedy. There were precedents enough. In his 1667 rewrite of *The Tempest*, Dryden, working in collaboration with Sir William Davenant, had given Miranda, Prospero's only child, a sister, and had added a boy who had never seen a woman. In 1678, in the prologue to his revision of *Timon of Athens*, Shadwell had praised Shakespeare's inimitable hand 'which never made more masterly strokes than in this'. But he could not forbear to add: 'Yet I can truly say, I have made it into a play'.

Tate's approach was much the same. It was, he claimed, his zeal for Shakespeare that had persuaded him to carry out the work; but having started on it he soon found that 'he had seized a treasure'. So *King Lear* was fitted out with a happy ending. The king regained both his sanity and his crown, his wretched daughters died of poison, and his loving daughter Cordelia was not allowed to die; instead she married Edgar, the faithful son of Lear's old friend, the duke of Gloucester. As for the Fool, he was eliminated. Tate did his work so well, in fact, that his adaptation became the definitive acting version for nearly 150 years. Dr Johnson certainly approved. In his edition of Shakespeare, published in 1765, he confessed that he had for years been too shocked by Cordelia's death to read again the closing scenes of the play.

Now 30 years old and an acknowledged Tory, Tate was asked by Dryden to collaborate on a sequel to *Absalom and Achitophel.* The new poem ran to 1,140 lines, of which only 200, including those describing Shadwell, were written by Dryden, though, no doubt, he revised the poem as a whole. For the next few years Tate and Dryden seem to have remained colleagues, the younger man helping with translations from Ovid, Juvenal, and Lucian.

Ever since the Restoration, in 1660, England had been going through a period of rapid social change. This was especially apparent in the theatre, where the typical audience no longer consisted of pleasure-loving courtiers, their interests confined to heroic tragedy and the so-called comedy of manners. Bourgeois values, based on the growing importance of trade and industry, were asserting themselves; and managers began to see the commercial attractions of farce. Audiences, moreover, preferred to have the great comic writers of the past, such as Molière and Jonson, presented to them in adaptations, much as people today prefer to watch, say, Dickens on television rather than read the original novel.

Tate's comedy, *A Duke and No Duke* (1684), was one of the milestones in this development of farce. The plot turns on a case of mistaken identity—a low-class character being confused with a duke, who happens to be abroad. But when he returns unexpectedly, the duke produces chaos as he countermands the orders given by his double.

As a full-time professional author, Tate produced a steady output including more adaptations from Jacobean plays, and a translation of a popular Latin history of plants which had been written by the poet Abraham Cowley (1618–67). More unusual perhaps was his *Syphilis: or, a Poetical History of the French disease*. Published in 1686, this was based on a medical poem written in Latin by Girolamo Fracastoro (1483–1553), an Italian physician. Fracastoro had named the disease after Syphilus, the shepherd-hero of his poem.

In 1689 Tate, working with the distinguished composer Henry Purcell (1659–95), made a remarkably successful venture into the field of opera, now established as an extremely popular form of entertainment. Purcell (who wrote the incidental music for some 40 plays during the last six years of his short life) had been commissioned to produce an occasional piece for an end-of-term function at a girl's school in Chelsea. *Dido and Aeneas*, the result of their collaboration, is now regarded as Purcell's operatic masterpiece. But at the time it was a once-only event, and it was not in fact produced again for another two centuries. Tate supplied the 'book', using his first play, *Brutus of Alba*, for source material. He proved to be a first-class librettist, with a really skilful knowledge of practical theatre.

In December 1692, a few weeks after the death of Shadwell, Tate was appointed poet laureate thanks to the earl of Dorset, his patron, who had become lord chamberlain on the accession of William III. But the office of laureate was no longer combined with that of historiographer royal. That post went to the critic Thomas Rymer (1641–1713), together with the salary of £200, and Tate himself had to be content with the annual fee of £100. The time for obligatory official odes by the laureate had not yet arrived—that had to wait until 1714 and the accession of George I, the first Hanoverian king. Nevertheless, Tate rapidly provided a poem for 1 January 1693, the first of about a dozen new year and birthday odes that flowed from his pen.

Tate seems to have felt that, by virtue of his office, he should respond to particular public occasions. Among the non-calendar events he chose to celebrate were, for instance, the new Parliament of 1701; the victories of 1704 against the French—which included the battle of Blenheim and the capture of Gibraltar; the Act of Union (1707) whereby England and Scotland became one kingdom; the further victories of 1708—the occupation of Minorca and Sardinia, and the battle of Oudenarde; and the signing of the Peace of Utrecht with France in 1713, which secured the Hanoverian succession in the United Kingdom.

Panacea, his poem in praise of tea ('The sovereign drink of pleasure and of health'), had of course nothing to do with his official duties as laureate. But such an original choice of subject shows how closely he must have followed changes in popular taste and fashion. When tea first appeared in London in the 1650s, it had been extremely expensive—more than £3 a pound, an enormous sum. But by 1700, when Tate's poem was published, tea was coming direct from China instead of via Holland, and the price had fallen to £1. No doubt, he and his publisher sensed they were on to a winner—even though the same amount of money would buy about eight pounds of tobacco from Virginia.

Although Tate continued to publish right up to the end of his life, including a long poem in memory of Queen Anne, who died in August 1714, his remaining years were marked by extreme poverty. Finally he was forced to seek shelter in the Mint, in Southwark, a place where debtors were legally protected from arrest. He died there on 30 July 1715—two months after the publication of his last official work, a song for George I's birthday—and lies buried nearby in St George's Church.

For the King's Birthday 1697

By September 1697 England was once again at peace with France—thanks to the exercise of British sea power. It was a subject for 'the utmost liberties of poetry' said Tate in his note introducing the joint publication of the birthday poem for 1697 and his next new year ode. The treaty brought to an end eight years of war in which Britain and the Netherlands had been allied with Austria and Spain. As a result, France yielded all the territory it had taken since 1679 (except Strasbourg and Landau), but got back Nova Scotia and the possessions it had lost in India. In return, Louis XIV recognized William III as king of England, a crushing blow for James II, the 'king over the water', although when James died four years later, Louis at once acknowledged his 13-year-old son as James III. The importance of having a strong navy was now fully understood, and thus emerged that great principle of British foreign policy—the need to prevent any major continental power holding the strategic area now occupied by Belgium and the Netherlands.

Summon to the cheerful plain
    The Graces and the Muses' train.

They come, they come, in pompous throng,
And, as in state they march along,
This is the burthen of their song:

Chorus
Virtue is at last regarded,
And the hero's toils rewarded.

    Hark how the neighb'ring nations round
To Britain's echo'd mirth resound!
And various languages employ
To speak the universal joy.

Let winter smile, the fields be gay,
   Woods and vales in consort sing,
   Flowing tides their tribute bring,
To welcome peace and Caesar's day.

The trumpet's sound and cannon's roar,
   No longer are the voice of war;
   Yet both shall speak, and both be heard as far
In triumph now as in alarms before.

   In ancient times of lawless sway,
When nations groaning lay,
Despairing all, and all forlorn,
Then was the great Alcides born.

   Such was Europe's late distress,
When for the suffering world's repose,
   With equal courage and success,
Our second Hercules arose.

   O favour'd both of earth and Heav'n!
To thee, and only thee, 'tis giv'n
Rome's first Caesars to out-do;
Our Julius and Augustus too.

War's dismal scene is chang'd to peace,
Yet shall not his Herculean labours cease:
   Nobler wars he now will wage,
   Against infernal pow'rs engage,
   And quell the hydra-vices of the age.

Grand chorus

   So glorious a task does a hero require,
Whom valour and virtue alike do inspire:
'Tis a triumph reserv'd for the just and the brave,
Who fights to give freedom, and conquers to save.

For New Year's Day 1698

Music now thy charms display,
   Let all thy tuneful sons appear,
To entertain the genial day,
And kindly treat the infant-year.

   Young as 'tis, it brings along
Blessings on its tender wing;
   Blessings to require your song;
Blessings that forestall the spring.

Chorus

The promis'd year is now arriv'd,
That has the golden age reviv'd.

   The prize our daring warrior sought
Is now completely gain'd;
   Not poorly begg'd, nor dearly bought,
But nobly, in the field, obtain'd.

Peace herself could boast no charms
To draw our hero from alarms,
   From glorious danger—till she came
   In honour's recommending name,
   And all the splendid pomp of fame.

Bellona else had still been heard,
   Thundering through the listed plain;
   Europe still, with restless pain,
Had for her fearless champion fear'd.

Harrass'd nations, now at rest,
   Echo to each other's joy,
   Their breath in grateful songs employ,
For him who has their griefs redrest.

Chorus

What then should happy Britain do?
Blest with the gift and giver too.

On warlike enterprizes bent
To foreign fields the hero went;
  The dreadful part he there perform'd
  Of battles fought, and cities storm'd:
But now the drum and trumpet cease,
  And wish'd success his sword has sheath'd,
  To us returns, with olive wreath'd,
To practice here the milder arts of peace.

Grand chorus

  Happy, happy, past expressing,
Britain, if thou know'st thy blessing;
Home-bred discord ne'er alarm thee,
Other mischief cannot harm thee.
Happy, if thou know'st thy blessing.
Happy, happy, past expressing.

For New Year's Day 1703

This is the first official poem Tate produced for Queen Anne, who came to the throne in March 1702. When he wrote it, England had been at war with France for eight months; but he chose to ignore the fighting and concentrated on conventional expressions of loyalty. Anne was the younger daughter of James II, and, like her elder sister Mary, she was a determined Protestant. In 1683 she married Prince George of Denmark, bearing him 17 children, none of whom survived for long. When war was resumed with France, soon after she became queen, she appointed John Churchill commander-in-chief; his wife Sarah had been her favourite attendant for more than 20 years. By the end of 1702 he had scored a number of victories against the French and was created duke of Marlborough.

Hark, how the Muses call aloud,
  To welcome Father Janus home;
  With double honour proud,
Double triumphs now allow'd,
For mighty blessings past, and greater yet to come.

They call, and bid the spring appear,
With wreaths of never-fading flow'rs,
Gather'd from Elysian bow'rs,
  Ever fragrant, ever gay,
  To crown the new auspicious day,
The smiling promise of a joyful year.

Chorus

Come Goddess of the spring, appear
With wreaths of ever smiling flow'rs,
Gather'd from Elysian bow'rs,
To crown the day that crowns the year.

Like you (the Goddess thus replies)
This young auspicious day I prize,
  But one more blest is drawing near;
  Till then, my infant-sweets must sleep,
  And I my fragrant glories keep
For Anna's royal day; 'tis that which crowns the year.

Sound the loudest trumpet, fame,
The joyful jubilee proclaim,
Through Europe's sighing plains,
  And nations long opprest;
  Tell 'em Britain's Anna reigns,
Britannia's Anna reigns, and Europe shall have rest.

War's angry voice be heard no more,
For joy alone the cannon roar;
For bloody bays, with gilded palm

Thy cradle infant-year be dress'd,
Thy cheerful days all halcyon calm;
Calm as Anna's sacred breast.

Thus let thy happy minutes glide,
In joy's uninterrupted tide;
And thy blest season, like the past,
A bright example give
To after-years; while time shall last,
While time shall last, and Anna's glory live.

Fame and fortune ever smile
On Britain's queen and Britain's isle:
Plenty springing through the plain;
Traffic floating on the main:
Peace at home; and, all abroad;
Oppressors quell'd; and tyrants aw'd.

With thousand thousand blessings more,
For sov'reign virtue kept in store,
To signalize the glorious reign:

Grand chorus

All that you can happy call,
On Anna and her royal consort fall,
The prince of early fame,
Illustrious as his name
England's protecting George, and guardian of the main.

For the King's Birthday 1715

This poem, his first ode addressed to the new monarch, George I, was the last to come from Tate, who died two months after the king's birthday. Until he succeeded Queen Anne in 1714, George, who was elector of Hanover, had never set foot in England, and his knowledge of English was poor. But he was a Protestant and therefore acceptable. The 'glorious heir' was the prince of Wales, on bad terms with his father, whom he eventually succeeded in 1727.

Arise harmonious pow'rs
From your Elysian bow'rs;
And nymphs Heliconian springs,
To caress the royal day,
That such a blessing did convey,
No less a blessing than the best of kings.

Yet, in the transport of your joys,
Beware the sacrilegious crime
Of trespassing upon the monarch's time,
Which since for common welfare he employs,
The muses' tribe would wrong
The public int'rest to detain him long.

Only to Britannia say,
Her happy days commence again,
That all her sorrows shall repay
And rescue her renown,
Since glorious George accepts the British crown
And kindly condescends to reign.

When kings that make the public good their care
Advance in dignity and state,
Their rise no envy can create,
Because their subjects in the grandeur share
For, like the sun, the higher they ascend
The farther their indulgent beams extend.

Yet long before our Royal Sun
His destined course has run
We're blest to see a glorious heir
That shall the mighty loss repair,
When he that blazes now, shall this low sphere resign,
In a sublimer orb eternally to shine.

A Cynthia too, adorned with ev'ry grace
   Of person and of mind;
And happy in a starry race
   Of such auspicious kind,
      As joyfully pressage
No want of royal heirs in any future age.

Chorus

Honoured with the best of kings,
And a set of lovely springs
From the royal fountain flowing;
Lovely streams can enter growing,
Happy Britain past expressing:
Only know to prize the blessing.

[4]
Nicholas Rowe
(1674–1718)

Nicholas Rowe was the first person to think of printing each of Shakespeare's plays with its own list of characters, and with the text divided into acts, scenes, and locations. But these innovations, which he introduced in 1709, when he himself had also become famous as a dramatist, were so simple and yet so obvious hardly anyone now remembers or recognizes what he did.

Born on 20 June 1674 at Little Barford, Bedfordshire, Nicholas was the eldest child of John and Elizabeth Rowe. His father, who came from Devon, was a barrister of the Middle Temple in London, and eventually became a serjeant-at-arms, the 17th-century equivalent of a queen's counsel. When Nicholas was five, his mother died. Like Dryden before him he was educated at Westminster School, where the formidable Dr Robert Busby (1606–95) was still headmaster. It was Dr Busby who had refused to doff his hat when Charles II visited the school: 'No boy must think there is anyone higher than his Master'.

Nicholas left Westminster in 1691, when he was just 17, to become a student at the Middle Temple. Less than a year later, his father died, leaving him £300 and his chambers in the Temple. The young man was eventually called to the bar, and started to practise. But apparently he soon forsook law for authorship. The muses, said an early biographer, 'had stolen away his heart from his infancy, and his passion for them rendered the study of the law dry and tasteless to his palate'. In 1698 he married Antonia Parsons, and their son John was born a year later.

Rowe's first play, *The Ambitious Stepmother*, a tragedy in blank verse, was produced early in 1700. It was based on a romantic drama by the Jacobean author Philip Massinger. The cast included three leading players of the time—Thomas Betterton, a former protégé of Sir William Davenant; Anne Bracegirdle, with whom Rowe is said to have fallen in love; and Elizabeth Barry, one-time mistress of the notorious earl of Rochester. The play itself was so well received, Rowe could now safely devote himself to the theatre. The taste for heroics was dying; audiences were beginning to prefer writers who appealed to their sense of pity.

Rowe's next play, *Tamerlane* produced at the end of 1701, was a very different type of tragedy. Although based on the great Tartar conqueror, it was essentially a political declaration. *Tamerlane* was intended as a compliment to William III (who died not long after the play opened), so he had to be presented as a constitutional monarch; while his rival, who represented Louis XIV, could be shown only as a despot. So well did the play capture the popular mood it became traditional to stage it on 5 November, the anniversary of William's landing in England.

In 1703 came *The Fair Penitent*, the first of Rowe's domestic, blank-verse 'she-tragedies' (the term was his own), which established him as a leading playwright. It dealt with what the author called 'a melancholy tale of private woes', and his success in portraying 'men and women as they are' to the new middle classes influenced the writing of tragedy for decades to come. The two other she-tragedies—*Jane Shore* (1714) and *Lady Jane Grey* (1715)—are constructed on much the same lines. Each contains melodramatic scenes carefully designed to arouse pity; and each requires an actress of passion to play the heroine. Decades later *The Fair Penitent* was still playing to full houses: David Garrick (1717–79) often acted the part of 'the haughty, gallant, gay Lothario', every woman's ideal of the handsome betrayer.

With three successful tragedies behind him, Rowe now turned to comedy. But when *The Biter* was produced in 1704, despite a prologue spoken by Betterton and an epilogue from Mrs Bracegirdle, it was a complete flop. Only the author enjoyed it; he is said to have roared with laughter at his own jokes. As a professional, however, he didn't quarrel with the popular verdict. Instead, he wrote a new tragedy, *Ulysses*, which had a successful reception in 1705. A few weeks later Rowe's wife died.

His next drama *The Royal Convert*, was set in Saxon England.

The play, which was produced in November 1707, contained some lines foretelling the blessings that would flow when England and Scotland were united (the actual event, in fact, had taken place that May). Rowe's gesture soon paid off, it seems, for in February 1709 he was appointed under secretary for Scotland. He held the post for two years, until his minister (and patron), the duke of Queensberry, who had carried through the treaty negotiations, suddenly died.

Although he devoted a lot of energy to the theatre, Rowe read widely in the classics, contributed to a number of translations, and was familiar with the literature of France, Italy, and Spain. He also produced occasional verse. In 1707, for instance, he celebrated the duke of Marlborough's victories on the continent, which included Blenheim (1704) and Ramillies (1706).

In 1709 Rowe produced his six-volume *Works of William Shakespear*. Not only was he the first person to undertake a serious editorial appraisal of the text, he also provided the first substantial 'account of the life and writings of the author'. This included various oddments of tradition as well as material supplied by Betterton, who had visited Stratford in order to collect whatever local information survived 90 years after Shakespeare's death. Drawing on his working knowledge of the theatre, Rowe was able—also for the first time—to provide each play with its list of characters; to divide the text into acts, scenes, and locations; to indicate entrances and exits. In addition, he modernized punctuation, spelling, and grammar, and corrected individual words and lines. Of course, without realizing it, he made it difficult for readers to appreciate the acting and printing conventions of Shakespeare's day; but the advantages of his work far outweighed the disadvantages.

Although Restoration and later dramatists regarded Shakespeare as an inexhaustible quarry, most of them had a great deal of respect for his work. In Dryden's adaptation of *Troilus and Cressida*, for instance, the prologue is spoken by the ghost of Shakespeare, who demands:

> Now, where are the successors to my name?
> What bring they to fill out a poet's fame?

Weak, short-lived issues of a feeble age;
Scarce living to be christened on the stage!

By the time Rowe's edition was published, something like ten per cent of all productions in London were either Shakespeare plays or adaptations.

Rowe obviously made the most of his Queensberry connection, for early in 1714 he dedicated his next play, *The Tragedy of Jane Shore*, to the new duke. He claimed to have written it in imitation of Shakespeare; but, as Dr Johnson said, they had little in common except a story that was English and some characters that were historical. (Jane Shore was the mistress of Edward IV.) The following year Rowe produced his *Tragedy of Lady Jane Grey*, which turned out to be his last work for the stage. He dedicated it to the princess of Wales, who had come to live in England with her husband in 1714, when Queen Anne died and George I succeeded. She and the prince had gathered a number of distinguished people round them, including Alexander Pope, who was a close friend of Rowe. This link proved useful, for a year or two later the prince of Wales appointed Rowe clerk of his council.

On 12 August 1715 Rowe became poet laureate in succession to Nahum Tate, who had died on 30 July; and later that year he was made land surveyor of customs in the port of London. His first new year ode duly appeared the following January, his first birthday ode at the end of May. Henceforth, laureates would have to justify their existence whenever January and the monarch's birthday came round.

In May 1718 the earl of Macclesfield, the new lord chancellor, made Rowe clerk of the presentation, another lucrative appointment; but as the laureate had only seven months to live, the post could have brought him little benefit. He died on 6 December 1718, leaving a widow, Anne, whom he had married in 1715, and a daughter of a few months; his only son John was by now 19. A few weeks later appeared what Dr Johnson called 'one of the greatest productions of English poetry'—Rowe's translation of the *Pharsalia*, an epic poem by the Roman poet Lucan. In her preface to this posthumous work, which was dedicated to George I, Anne Rowe claimed that her husband had always intended it to be a tribute to the king. She received in due course an annual pension of £40.

Rowe was buried in Poet's Corner, Westminster Abbey, close to the tomb of Dryden. Compared with earlier laureates, he had attracted little abuse. But then, as his friend and physician, Dr James Welwood, wrote, he had an 'inimitable manner of diverting and enlivening the company [which] made it impossible for any one to be out of humour when he was in it'.

For the New Year 1716

By the time Rowe's first ode for George I was ready for performance, the monarch had left England on a visit to Hanover, although the Jacobite rising in Scotland had only just been put down—'Faction, Fury, all are fled'. such was the antipathy between the king and the prince of Wales, George had refused to nominate his son as regent during his absence, preferring to revive the archaic title of 'Guardian of the Realm and Lieutenant'. As the laureate reminds his audience, which included the prince of Wales and his wife, Caroline of Ansbach, the prince had fought bravely at Oudenarde (Audenard) one of Marlborough's victories over the French.

Hail to thee, glorious rising Year,
With what uncommon grace thy days appear!
Comely art thou in thy prime,
Lovely child of hoary Time;
Where thy golden footsteps tread,
Pleasures all around thee spread;
Bliss and beauty grace thy train;
Muse, strike the lyre to some immortal strain.
But, oh! what skill, what master hand,
Shall govern or constrain the wanton band?
Loose like my verse they dance, and all without command.
Images of airest things
Crowd about the speaking strings;
Peace and sweet prosperity,
Faith and cheerful loyalty,
With smiling love and deathless poesy.

Ye scowling shades who break away,
Well do ye fly and shun the purple day,
Every fiend and fiend-like form,
Black and sullen as a storm,
Jealous Fear, and false Surmise,
Danger with her dreadful eyes,
Faction, Fury, all are fled,
And bold Rebellion hides her daring head.
Behold, thou gracious Year, behold,
To whom thy treasures all thou shalt unfold,
For whom thy whiter days were kept from times of old!
See thy George, for this is he!
On his right hand waiting free,
Britain and fair Liberty,
Every good is in his face,
Every open honest grace.
Thou great Plantagenet; immortal be thy race!

See! the sacred scion springs,
See the glad promise of a line of kings!
Royal youth! what bard divine,
Equal to a praise like thine,
Shall in some exalted measure
Sing thee, Britain's dearest treasure?
Who her joy in thee shall tell,
Who the sprightly note shall swell,
His voice attempering to the tuneful shell?
Thee Audenard's recorded field,
Bold in thy brave paternal band, beheld,
And saw with hopeless heart thy fainting rival yield:
Troubled he, with sore dismay,
To thy stronger fate gave way,
Safe beneath thy noble scorn,
Wingy-footed was he borne,
Swift as the fleeting shades upon the golden corn.

What valour, what distinguish'd worth,
From thee shall lead the coming ages forth?
Crested helms and shining shields,
Warriors fam'd in foreign fields;
Hoary heads with olive bound,
Kings and lawgivers renown'd;
Crowding still they rise anew,
Beyond the reach of deep prophetic view.
Young Augustus! never cease!
Pledge of our present and our future peace,
Still pour the blessings forth, and give thy great increase.
All the stock that fate ordains
To supply succeeding reigns,
Whether glory shall inspire
Gentler arts or martial fire,
Still the fair descent shall be
Dear to Albion, all, like thee,
Patrons of righteous rules, and foes to tyranny.

Ye golden lights who shine on high,
Ye potent planets who ascend the sky,
On the opening year dispense
All your kindest influence;
Heavenly powers be all prepar'd
For our Carolina's guard;
Short and easy be the pains,
Which for a nation's weal the heroine sustains.
Britannia's angel, be thou near
The growing race is thy peculiar care,
Oh spread thy sacred wing above the royal fair.
George by thee was wafted o'er
To the long expected shore:
None presuming to withstand
Thy celestial armed hand,
While his sacred head to shade,
The blended cross on high thy silver shield display'd.

But, oh! what other form divine,
Propitious near the hero seems to shine!
Peace of mind, and joy serene,
In her sacred eyes are seen,
Honour binds her mitred brow,
Faith and truth beside her go,
With zeal and pure devotion bending low.
A thousand storms around her threat,
A thousand billows roar beneath her feet,
While, fixed upon a rock, she keeps her stable seat.
Still in sign of sure defence,
Trust and mutual confidence,
On the monarch, standing by,
Still she bends her gracious eye,
Nor fears her foes' approach, while Heaven and he are nigh.

Hence then with every anxious care!
Be gone, pale Envy, and thou, cold Despair!
Seek ye out a moody cell,
Where Deceit and Treason dwell;
There repining, raging, still
The idle air with curses fill;
There blast the pathless wild, and the bleak northern hill;
There your exile vainly moan;
There where, with murmurs horrid as your own,
Beneath the sweeping winds, the bending forests groan,
But thou, Hope, with smiling cheer,
Do thou bring the ready year;
See the Hours! a chosen band!
See with jocund looks they stand,
All in their trim array, and waiting for command.

The welcome train begins to move,
Hope leads increase and chaste connubial love:
Flora sweet her bounty spreads,
Smelling gardens, painted meads;

Ceres crowns the yellow plain;
Pan rewards the shepherd's pain;
All is plenty, all is wealth,
And on the balmy air sits rosy-colour'd health.
I hear the mirth, I hear the land rejoice,
Like many waters swells the pealing noise,
While to their monarchs, thus, they raise the public voice.
'Father of thy country, hail!
Always every where prevail;
Pious, valiant, just, and wise,
Better suns for thee arise,
Purer breezes fan the skies,
Earth in fruits and flowers is drest,
Joy abounds in every breast,
For thee thy people all, for thee the year is blest.'

For the King's Birthday 1716

Rowe's ode for George I's 56th birthday sticks firmly to conventional compliments and pleasantries. It illustrates how emphasis has already shifted away from direct involvement with contemporary affairs towards the safety of routine flattery. One can only wonder how he would have handled the execution of Jacobite rebels or the passing of an act extending the maximum duration of Parliament to seven years—just two events that had occurred since the publication of his ode for the new year.

Lay thy flowery garlands by,
Ever-blooming gentle May!
Other honours now are nigh;
Other honours see we pay,
Lay thy flowery garlands by, etc.

Majesty and great renown
Wait thy beamy brow to crown.
Parent of our hero, thou,
George on Britain didst bestow.

Thee the trumpet, thee the drum,
With the plumy helm, become:
Thee the spear and shining shield,
With every trophy of the warlike field.

Call thy better blessings forth,
For the honour of his birth:
Still the voice of loud commotion,
Bid complaining murmurs cease,
Lays the billows of the ocean;
And compose the land in peace.
Call thy better, etc.

Queen of odours, fragrant May,
For this boon, this happy day,
Janus with the double face
Shall to thee resign his place,
Thou shalt rule with better grace:
Time from thee shall wait his doom,
And thou shalt lead the year for every age to come.

Fairest month, in Caesar pride thee,
Nothing like him canst thou bring,
Though the graces smile beside thee:
Though thy bounty gives the Spring.

Though like Flora thou array thee,
Finer than the painted bow;
Carolina shall repay thee
All thy sweetness, all thy show.

She herself a glory greater
Than thy golden sun discloses;
And her smiling offspring sweeter
Than the bloom of all thy roses.

For the King's Birthday 1718

Rowe portrays George I as a great peacemaker, 'author of the world's repose', for 1717 had brought into being the so-called Triple Alliance. This united Britain, France, and the Netherlands as a group to block Spanish efforts to dominate events in central Europe. The alliance was extended in the summer of 1718 to include Austria, which had recently defeated a large Turkish army near Belgrade.

Oh touch the string, celestial Muse, and say,
Why are peculiar times and seasons blest?
Is it in fate, that one distinguish'd day
Should with more hallow'd purple paint the east?

Look on life and nature's race!
How the careless minutes pass,
How they wear a common face:
One is what another was!
Till the happy hero's worth
Bid the festival stand forth;
Till the golden light he crown,
Till he mark it for his own.

How had this glorious morning been forgot,
Unthought of as the things that never were;
Had not our greatest Caesar been its lot,
And call'd it from amongst the vulgar year!

Now, Nature, be gay
In the pride of thy May,
To court let thy graces repair;
Let Flora bestow
The crown from her brow,
For our brighter Britannia to wear.

Through every language of thy peopled earth,
Far as the sea's or Caesar's influence goes,
Let thankful nations celebrate his birth,
And bless the author of the world's repose.

Let Volga tumbling in cascades,
  And Po that glides through poplar shades,
  And Tagus bright in sands of gold,
  And Arethusa, rivers old,
    Their great deliverer sing.
Not, Danube, thou whose winding flood
So long has blush'd with Turkish blood,
To Caesar shall refuse a strain,
Since now thy streams without a stain
    Run crystal as their spring.

Chorus

To mighty George, that heals thy wounds,
That names thy kings and marks thy bounds,
The joyful voice, O Europe, raise:
In the great mediator's praise
Let all thy various tongues combine,
And Britain's festival be thine.

[5]
Laurence Eusden
(1688–1730)

Laurence Eusden had the misfortune to be described, in 1757, as a drunken parson by so notable a writer as Thomas Gray, author of the famous *Elegy in a Country Churchyard*. The remark occurs in a letter Gray wrote turning down the laureateship, which had been offered to him when Colley Cibber died—Gray was in somewhat censorious mood at the time; the same letter refers to the 'disgraceful' character of Dryden. Discussing previous holders of the office, he remarked: 'Eusden was a person of great hopes in his youth, though at last he turned out a drunken parson.' His reputation has suffered accordingly, but, surely, it's the first half of this comment that is significant, for it provides reliable evidence of the positive way in which Eusden's contemporaries regarded him when he was a young man. Between the age of 23 and 24, for instance, he was writing occasional pieces for the *Spectator*, a daily periodical written by Joseph Addison and Richard Steele, which appeared between 1711 and 1712, and again in 1714. Steele in fact names Eusden as one of a number of writers who had made important contributions to the *Spectator* during its first year of publication.

Eusden was born at Spofforth, Yorkshire (about five miles from Harrogate), where his father, who bore the same name, was vicar. He was baptized on 6 September 1688, two months before the arrival in England of William of Orange, the future William III, an event that soon brought about the end of Dryden's tenure of office as first poet laureate. Educated at St Paul's School, York, until he was 16½, he went up to Trinity College, Cambridge, in 1705 as a commoner. His academic ability soon led to recognition, for he was appointed a scholar of the college within six months. In 1708 he graduated, becoming a minor fellow three years later and a full fellow and lecturer in 1712.

It is important to stress Eusden's youthful abilities, because very few facts are known about his life, and—all too often—these have been used to discredit him. In 1712, when Eusden became a fellow of Trinity, Richard Bentley, the greatest classical scholar of his time and a pioneer of the subtle art of textual criticism, had been Master of the college for 12 years. Bentley's success in reforming the abuses, financial and otherwise, that were widespread within the college, to say nothing of his outstanding academic ability, had naturally made him exceptionally unpopular. Indeed, in 1710, the fellows had tried, unsuccessfully, to have him ejected from the mastership—one stage in a dispute that was to last almost another 30 years. It seems unlikely that such a hard-headed—if thoroughly irascible—crusader and fellow-Yorkshireman would have approved the election of a non-entity to the governing body of his college.

In 1717 Eusden was one of nine contributors to a 15-volume translation of Ovid's *Metamorphoses*. Once again, he was in good company, for the translators included such famous writers as Dryden (by now dead), Addison, John Gay (author of the *Beggar's Opera*, 1728), and the dramatist William Congreve, (author of *Love for Love*). Addison and Congreve had other claims to literary fame, for like Sir Samuel Garth, the book's editor, they were members of the Kit-Cat Club, whose secretary was Jacob Tonson, the most famous publisher of his time. The members of this distinguished literary/political society at one time included politicians such as Sir Robert Walpole and the duke of Marlborough, as well as writers like Steele and Sir John Vanbrugh. The involvement of Jacob Tonson is particularly significant. Born in 1656, he had issued most of Dryden's works, and had been joint publisher of the *Spectator*. More particularly, in 1709 he had published Eusden's earliest printed work *Hero and Leander*, a translation from the Greek, which had appeared in one of his poetical miscellanies.

In 1714, when Queen Anne died and was succeeded by George I, the elector of Hanover, a German prince who never learned to speak English, Eusden published a celebratory poem, *The Royal Family!—A Letter to Mr Addison on the King's Accession to the Throne*. It received a commendary notice in the *Spectator*. Perhaps emboldened by this success, Eusden now decided the time had come to acquire a patron. According to the custom and practice of the day, he needed an influential person to support him or to help him to find some form of lucrative employment. He set his sights therefore on Charles Montagu, who had been made first earl of Halifax and principal minister, (in effect, prime minister, though the title was not yet in use) on the accession of George I. To that end, Eusden turned into Latin a poem written some years earlier by Halifax on the battle of the Boyne, William III's victory in Ireland over James II. In addition, he addressed a poem in English to Halifax himself. There was, of course, nothing unusual in such an attempt to gain recognition, and in the ordinary course of events he might well have succeeded. But Halifax died suddenly in 1715, aged 53, and Eusden had to look elsewhere. Eventually, he turned his attention to Lord Thomas Pelham-Holles, at 22 one of the greatest landowners in England, who had been made duke of Newcastle in 1715. At a time when half the Church of England livings were worth less than £50 a year, the duke's annual income totalled at least £40,000. When the duke married on 2 April 1717, Eusden sent him an elaborate poem in celebration of the occasion. This time he was successful. In December the following year Nicholas Rowe, the poet laureate, died, and the duke rewarded Eusden with the post, which was in his gift as lord chamberlain. Eusden had gained the approval of one of the most influential men in England. Newcastle had already been instrumental in securing the support for George I of the city of London when he became king; and for the next 50 years he controlled the elaborate apparatus of patronage that sustained the whole process of so-called parliamentary government in England.

In his *Lives of the Poets* (1753) Theophilus Cibber, son of Colley Cibber, said that Newcastle could not have made a better choice:

> We shall have occasion to find, as we enumerate his writings, that he was no inconsiderable versifier, and though perhaps he had not the brightest parts; yet as we hear of no moral blemish imputed to him, and as he was dignified with holy-orders, his grace acted a very generous part, in providing for a man who had conferred an obligation on him. The first rate poets were either of principles very different

> from the government, or thought themselves too distinguished to undergo the drudgery of an annual Ode; and in this case Eusden seems to have had as fair a claim as another . . .

Eusden was only 30 when he became poet laureate, which makes him the youngest poet ever to win the appointment, a distinction worthy of mention. Significantly, too, his four predecessors had all been dramatists and satirists, which helped to keep them in the public gaze. Eusden was neither.

The remaining 12 years of his life seem to have gone virtually unrecorded, so we may never know how the 'great hopes' of his youth were blasted. In 1719 he figures briefly in the duke of Buckingham's *Session of the Poets*, another pedestrian poem on the inevitable theme that all poets laureate are unskilled versifiers and beneath contempt. Buckingham, who built his home where the royal palace now stands, died in 1721; he was a friend of Pope and had been one of Dryden's patrons.

His fellowship at Trinity College must have expired by about 1719, because no fellow could continue as a member of the foundation if he were not ordained within seven years of his election, and —for some reason—Eusden did not choose to avail himself of the opportunity. In 1724, however, he changed his mind about entering the church and was ordained. This was apparently done because Richard, Lord Willoughby de Broke wanted to have him as his chaplain, an appointment he probably held for several years. But he could have been influenced by his involvement (from about 1720) with Mrs Crisp, a clergyman's daughter—whose whole family have been blamed for his eventual alcoholism. In May 1730 he was appointed rector of Coningsby, a remote village in Lincolnshire. He was only 42 when he died, a few months later, of dropsy.

During the 12 years of his laureateship, he had dutifully supplied his biannual quota of odes. Ironically, his last poem, an ode for George II's birthday, was performed in London on 30 October 1730. Next day there arrived news of his death, which had taken place a month before, on 27 September.

For the New Year 1720

Eusden's New Year Ode for 1720 is unabashed panegyric, the work of a man unwilling or unable to use his privileged position as laureate to comment on topical issues. No hint, therefore, in these three odes of the activities of the South Sea Company, the great talking point of 1719–20 in England. When speculation in the shares suddenly collapsed, thousands of people were ruined. Sir Robert Walpole's success in dealing with the crisis made Whig power secure for years, while George I, who had been Governor of the company, was especially grateful for the dextrous manner in which Walpole handled the cover-up.

The 1721 ode for the king's birthday contains a more original handling than usual of the conventional references to Caesar, who this time appears as a personage in his own right, to say nothing of the Druidic bard, an early presentation of a character that figured prominently as an ingredient of Romantic landscape. Like other writers of the period, Eusden uses Nassau as an epithet for William III (of the House of Orange-Nassau), and Brunswick for George I (of the House of Brunswick-Hanover).

The Carolina, 'fruitful mother of our joys', that Eusden invokes in his 1723 ode is the 40-year-old Caroline of Ansbach, the princess of Wales. She bore her husband, the future George II, eight children before she died in 1737.

Recitativo

Lift up thy hoary head, and rise
  Thou mighty Genius of this isle:
Around thee cast thy wond'ring eyes,
  See all thy Albion smile.
Mirth's goddess her blest pow'r maintains
In cities, courts, and rural plains,
Brunswick, the glorious Brunswick reigns.

Air

Tho' thy kind eyes were once o'erflowing,
Our too impending dangers knowing:
Tho' days, tho' nights were spent in groaning,
Poor Britannia's fate bemoaning:
Now forbear, forbear to languish,
Cheerful rise from needless anguish:
For pleasures now are ever growing,
Tho' thy kind eyes were once o'er-flowing.

Recitativo

Let the young, dawning year a George resound,
A George's fame can fill its spacious round.
Here ev'ry virtue pleas'd thou may'st behold,
Which rais'd a hero to a god of old.
To form this One the mix'd ideas draw
From Edward, Henry, and the lov'd Nassau.

Air

Such to Britannia is her king,
As the softly murmuring spring
To thirsty travellers, who sweat
On Libyan sands, and die with heat.
They view it with a glad surprise,
And drink the water with their eyes.
Then with gay hearts, refresh'd, they sing:
Such to Britannia is her king.

Recitativo

By thee contending nations are ally'd,
By thee, Hesperia sinks her tow'ring pride.
Moscovia's prince begins his bounds to know,
And roaring Volga silently to flow.
Thee Gallia's regent with fix'd eyes admires,
For thee Germania feels a lover's fires.
From Belgian moles thy praise is heard around,
Thy Albion's cliffs return the pleasing sound.
Janus again his iron doors must close,
A new Augustus seeks the world's repose.

Air

With raptures ev'ry breast is fir'd,
  Loud paeans ev'ry tongue employ;
Thus while great Jove sometimes retir'd,
  The court of gods his absence mourn'd,
  But when the Thunderer return'd,
The whole Olympus shook with joy.

Chorus

Genius! now securely rest,
We shall ever now be blest.
Thou thy guardianship may'st spare,
Britannia is a Brunswick's care.

For the King's Birthday 1721

Recitativo

When the great Julius on Britannia's strand
First leap'd, he cried, 'Thou sweet, delightful land!
'Tis Caesar tells thee, he must thee command.'
'Brave hero!' the pleas'd legions shout around;
'Brave hero!' all the list'ning cliffs resound:
'Thy equal in no future age shall rise:
One Caesar rule the earth, one Jove the skies!'

Air

Vales of pleasure are her vales,
Peaceful smile her silent dales.
Smoothly flow her crystal floods,
Verdant rise her shady woods.
Nor let fam'd Olympus dare
With Albion's mountains to compare:
Tho', big with fabl'd gods, he shrouds
His lofty head amid the clouds.

Recitativo

Straight from a hallow'd grove there sprung,
    Wreath'd with an acorn'd crown of oak,
The ruling Druid of the throng,
    And thus the hoary prophet spoke.

'Caesar! wilt thou lend an ear?
  Thou, the boasted pride of Rome!
Truths ungrateful cans't thou bear,
  And not tremble at thy doom?'

Air

The soldiers, with rash fury sir'd,
No foresight from the seer desir'd;
Not him, as sacred priest, rever'd,
Nor all his threatened dangers fear'd;
Swift had he felt a mangled death
For his mis-tim'd, prophetic breath:
But Caesar heard the whisper'd ruin run
Thro' all the cohorts, ere the crime was done;
  And with one awful, Roman look,
  Their impious conspiration broke,
  And silent, more than speaking, spoke:
  Then greatly bad the daring bard sing on.

Recitativo

  'Will wild ambition know no bound?'
    With heav'd up hands the Druid cried.
    'Thou, Caesar, now shin'st in thy pride;
  Thy conquests, warrior, are renown'd:
    Enough!—Would'st thou be deify'd?
Proud mortal, know!—the fatal Ides shall come,
When thou thyself shalt bleed for bleeding Rome.'

Air

'Tho' they flatt'ring minions tell thee,
None can rise who shall excel thee;
In revolving years, believe me
(Hero! I will not deceive thee)
From distant, German climes shall rise
A hero, more than Julius, wise;
More good, more prais'd, more truly great,
Courted to sway Britannia's state:

Such are the fix'd decrees of fate.'
The priest, the bard, the prophet then withdrew,
And to the thickest, sylvan covert flew.

Chorus

Britons! The promis'd blessing you behold,
So many finished centuries foretold.
Inhuman Caesar strove to chain mankind;
Your gen'rous monarch labours to unbind.
That, to himself with joy saw altars rais'd;
This, blushes even to hear his merit prais'd.
He owns his glories to the pow'r divine;
Asks but his people's love, and not a shrine.
Caesar records his fame from captive lands,
But George from rescued kingdoms his demands.
Europe's firm peace is now his glorious aim;
The love of peace from heav'n derives its flame:
Hush'd was the world when the Messiah came.

For the King's Birthday 1723

Recitativo

Hail to the lov'd, returning, glorious day!
Let Phoebus gild it with a brighter ray:
Long may we joy to see it smiling rise,
And long great Brunswick want his kindred skies.

Air

Breath the hautboy, touch the lyre,
Melting harmony inspire!
Let no clouded brow be found

In the glittering, pompous round.
Music! gently fan love's fire,
Welcome Mirth and young Desire,
Breath the hautboy, touch the lyre,
Melting harmony inspire!

Recitativo

To him, what numbers shall we bring,
In equal numbers, whom no muse can sing?
To him, what deathless trophy raise,
Who, all transcending, nobly scorns all praise?
In pleasing wonder lost we see,
How lovely virtue shines in Majesty!

Air

Still let nations, freed, resound him,
Guardian angels still surround him,
Crown him with the sweetest pleasure,
Without end, and without measure,
Let no treacherous foe confound him,
Still let nations, freed, resound him,
Guardian angels still surround him!

Recitativo

But hear! the yelling Furies rave;
How widely yawns th' Avernian cave!
See! Treason from the realms of night
Uprears her head, a hideous spright!
The monster, pale with guilty fears,
No sooner spy'd, but disappears.

Air

O! Traitors, odious train!
Of public bliss the bane!
With pious leer demure,
Fain would they stab secure.
An outward ease they wear,

But pant with inward care.
Their dreams new horrors bring,
They fly a vengeful king.
    O! Traitors, odious train!
    Of public bliss the bane!

Chorus

'Tis Carolina all their hopes destroys,
    The fruitful mother of our joys!
Still may the royal progeny appear
    Increas'd by ev'ry circling year;
Still let kind Heaven display each dark design,
    Shield Brunswick and his godlike line:
This we for blessings on Britannia pray,
    Britannia! ever blest, if they.

[6]
Colley Cibber
(1671–1757)

No laureate more richly deserves the title 'man of the theatre' than Colley Cibber. As comedian, dramatist, actor-manager, and impressario, his working life spanned some 55 years. But his supreme achievement is his vastly diverting autobiography, *An Apology for the Life of Mr Colley Cibber, Comedian*, which contains a store of invaluable information about the stage, from the Restoration onward.

Because Cibber paints such an honest self-portrait, we can see him more vividly than we can most other laureates. (Austin's autobiography is too discursive to have much value, while those of Masefield and Day-Lewis are incomplete.) Cibber, who had to endure more childish abuse than most laureates, and did so with much good humour, emerges as an engaging character. Indeed, one of his most likeable traits is his steadfast refusal to take the laureateship very seriously. If the king really wanted Colley, who never claimed to be a poet, to produce a brace of odes each year—and would give him £100 and a butt of wine for his pains—how absurd to refuse.

Cibber was born in London on 6 November 1671, the eldest son of Caius Gabriel Cibber, a distinguished Danish sculptor, much employed at Chatsworth, Derbyshire, which the duke of Devonshire had begun building in 1687. He was educated at Grantham, in Lincolnshire, not far from where his mother's family, the Colleys, lived. At 16 there were plans to send him to Winchester College; but when these fell through he was taken to London, where he soon became stagestruck. When William of Orange landed in England late in 1688, Colley, as anti-Catholic as his father, spent the winter as a volunteer, but of course saw no fighting. In 1690 he got a job at Drury Lane as an actor, and three years later had gained enough security to marry and start a family.

In 1696 Cibber's first play, *Love's Last Shift*, was performed at Drury Lane. Historically, the piece is important because it was one of the earliest so-called sentimental comedies. But most important of all, the play inspired John Vanbrugh (then 33) to write a sequel—his first play—*The Relapse, or Virtue in Danger*. Sir Novelty Fashion, the chief character, was renamed Lord Foppington, but the part continued to be taken by Cibber, who excelled at portraying coxcombs and other eccentrics.

In 1700 Cibber embarked on his first adaptation of Shakespeare, and his *Richard III*—half its 2,000-odd lines were his own—turned out to be as popular as Nahum Tate's version of *King Lear* had been, back in 1681. Undeniably, the result was a travesty. But it succeeded so well it became the standard acting text for the next 120 years. 'Off with his head! So much for Buckingham!', his most famous line, is in every good book of quotations.

By this time Cibber was taking an active interest in the business side of Drury Lane theatre, while continuing his acting and writing careers. In 1709, in company with two other players—Thomas Doggett, a character actor (and founder of a famous race still rowed each year on the Thames), and Robert Wilks, a light comedian—he became one of the joint managers of Drury Lane. Anne Oldfield, excellent in both comic and tragic roles, became their leading lady, and so began a period of prosperity that was to last for almost 20 years.

After the death of Queen Anne in 1714, Cibber became active in the world of politics, writing and adapting plays for the Whigs, the party that supported the new king, George I, founder of the Hanoverian dynasty. His *Non-Juror*, an anti-Catholic diatribe, produced at Drury Lane in 1717 was enormously successful, running for 16 nights. The play was based on Molière's *Tartuffe*, with Cibber himself taking the lead role, that of Dr Wolf, an English Catholic priest inciting others to rebellion. He received £200 from the king, to whom the piece was dedicated, and Nicholas Rowe, then poet laureate, supplied an appropriate prologue. Cibber always claimed that it was this play that eventually won him the laureateship in 1730; but by then he was one of the best-known theatrical figures in London.

The triumph of *The Non-Juror* compensated for the failure, earlier that year, of a promising farce called *Three Hours after Marriage*, for which the Drury Lane management must have had high hopes. Written by John Gay, with additional material supplied by his friend Alexander Pope, who was then 29, it had included a take-off of Cibber—played by Cibber himself—and some business with a mummy and a crocodile. The authors were extremely annoyed when the play had to be withdrawn. Cibber of course took the set-back in his stride, and soon followed it with a production of *The Rehearsal*, an old standby, into which he introduced some gags about the crocodile and the mummy. Pope, who was present at an early performance, became so furious he want backstage and picked a quarrel with Cibber. But the actor-manager, almost 18 years his senior, refused to make any cuts; and the following night he actually punched Gay, when he in turn came round to protest. It was the start of a long and famous literary feud between Cibber and Pope, who—himself a Catholic—had not been at all pleased about the success of *The Non-Juror*. (The term described clergymen who refused to take an oath of allegiance to George I.)

On 3 December 1730, two months after the death of Laurence Eusden, Cibber who was now 59, was appointed poet laureate, a post he was to hold for 27 years turning out odes with the minimum waste of time and effort. His chief rival for the laureateship had been Stephen Duck, a Wiltshire farm worker, whose verses had already so impressed Queen Caroline that she had awarded him a pension of £30 a year. Cibber's first official work, the New Year ode for 1731, spawned an unprecedented number of parodies, one of them written (under the name of Francis Fairplay) by the new laureate himself.

By the time he was 62, Cibber was getting ready to retire. He began the process by quitting the Drury Lane management, and thereafter took only the occasional stage role. This gave him plenty of time for his autobiography, which was published in 1740, when he was 69. Oliver Goldsmith, author of *The Vicar of Wakefield*, who was only ten when *The Apology* first appeared, later said of it: 'There are few who do not prefer a page of Montaigne or Colley Cibber, who candidly tell us what they thought of the world, or the world thought of them, to the more stately memoirs and transactions of Europe.'

Sporadic skirmishing with Pope continued over the years. But by 1742 Cibber had had enough, and published *A Letter from Mr Cibber to Mr Pope*. In it he freely admitted he was not a major literary figure, and wondered therefore why the greatest poet of the age should waste so much time on him. He even admitted to keeping company with lords and whores (an old accusation of Pope's). Warming to the subject, he went on to describe, with piquant detail, how he had once found Pope in a highclass brothel off the Haymarket. 'The little-tiny manhood of Mr Pope [he was only 4 ft 6 in tall] had been tempted into the next room', said Cibber, by the girl who served tea to clients, leaving the author and a young lord behind, anxious to learn what would happen. After a suitable pause, Cibber flung open the bedroom door, only to find 'this little hasty hero, like a terrible tomtit, pertly perched upon the mount of love'. Expressing concern lest the great translator of Homer should catch a malady from which he might not recover, the narrator boldly 'laid hold of his heels, and actually drew him down safe and sound from his danger'.

Pope could reply only by issuing yet another—the final—edition of his *Dunciad* (1743), with Cibber enthroned as the new prince of Dulness. But nobody could upstage the old actor; and when Pope died in May 1744 he provided a special epitaph, which appeared in the next issue of *The Gentleman's Magazine*.

Cibber made his final appearance the following year, playing in his own, highly original, version of Shakespeare's *King John*. Though 74 and without teeth, he insisted on going on; but the performance was not a success, particularly as David Garrick's production of the real *King John* was playing at a nearby theatre.

His official odes continued until he died, on 11 December 1757, at the age of 86. He was buried in Grosvenor Chapel, South Audley Street. Despite the many achievements of his long and eventful career, he could always take a disarming look at his own writing: 'No Man worthy the Name of an Author is a more faulty Writer than myself; that I am not Master of my own Language, I too often feel, when I am at a loss for Expression.'

For the New Year 1731

Although he was already 59 when he became laureate and had to all intents retired from acting, Cibber managed to produce a steady succession of new year and birthday odes until his death 27 years later. The three printed here, beginning with his first offering, are ample evidence of the mechanical methods he employed to fulfil his annual quota. Indeed, the ancient adage 'Don't get it right, get it written' might well have been coined expressly for the old actor-manager.

By now, too, the method of presenting the odes at St James's Palace, with music specially written by the Master of the King's Music, had become very much a standardized affair. Those concerned can have taken only the minimum of trouble with these productions, knowing that there would be no repeat performances to bother about.

Recitativo

Once more the ever-circling sun
   Thro' the celestial signs has run,
Again old Time inverts his glass,
And bids the annual seasons pass:
The youthful spring shall call for birth,
And glad with op'ning flow'rs the earth:
Fair summer load with sheaves the field,
And golden fruit shall autumn yield:
Each to the winter's want their store shall bring,
'Till warmer genial suns recall the spring.

Air

Ye grateful Britons bless the year,
   That kindly yields increase,
While plenty that might feed a war,
   Enjoys the guard of peace,
Your plenty to the skies you owe,
   Peace is your monarch's care,
Thus bounteous Jove and George below
   Divided empire share.

Recitativo

Britannia pleas'd, looks round her realms to see
Your various causes of felicity!
(To glorious war, a glorious peace succeeds;
For most we triumph when the farmer feeds)
Then truly are we great when truth supplies
Our blood, our treasures drain'd by victories.
Turn, happy Britons, to the throne your eyes,
And in the royal offspring see
How amply bounteous Providence supplies
The source of your felicity.

Air

Behold in ev'ry face imperial graces shine
All native to the race of George and Caroline
In each young hero we admire
The blooming virtues of his sire;
In each maturing fair we find
Maternal charms of softer kind.

Recitativo

In vain thro' ages past has Phoebus roll'd
Ere such a sight blest Albion could behold.
Thrice happy mortals, if your state you knew,
Where can the globe so blest a nation shew?
All that of you indulgent Heav'n requires,
Is loyal hearts, to reach your own desires.
Let faction then her self-born views lay down,
And hearts united, thus address the throne.

Air

Hail! royal Caesar, hail!
Like this may ev'ry annual sun
Add brighter glories to thy crown,
'Till suns themselves shall fail.

Recitativo

May Heav'n thy peaceful reign prolong,
Nor let to thy great empire's wrong,
Foreign or native foes prevail.
Hail, etc.

For the King's Birthday 1731

When Charles, from anarchy's retreat,
Resum'd the regal seat;
When (hence by frantic zealots driv'n)
Our holy Church, our Laws,
Returning, with the royal cause,
Rais'd up their thankful eyes, to Heaven,
Then hand in hand,
To bless the land,
Protection, with Obedience came,
And mild Oblivion wav'd Revenge,
For wrongs of civil flame.

Wild, and wanton, then, our joys,
Loud, as raging war before:
All was triumph, tuneful noise,
None, from Heaven, could hope for more.

Brother, son, and father foes,
Now embracing, bless their home:
Who so happy, could suppose
Happier days were still to come?

But Providence, that better knows
Our wants, than we,
Previous to those,
(Which human wisdom could not, then, forsee)
Did, from the pregnant former day,
A race of happier reigns, to come, convey.

The Sun, we saw precede,
Those mighty joys restor'd,
Gave to our future need,
From great Plantagenet a Lord;
From whose high veins this greater day arose,
A second George to fix our world's repose,
From Charles restor'd, short was our term of bliss,
But George from George entails our happiness.

From a heart which abhors the abuse of high pow'r,
Are our liberties duly defended;
From a courage, inflam'd by the terrors of war,
With his fame, is our commerce extended.
Let our public high spirits be rais'd, to their height
Yet our prince, in that virtue, will lead 'em.
From our welfare, he knows, that his glory's more bright;
As obedience enlarges our freedom.

What ties can bind a grateful people more,
That such diffus'd benevolence of pow'r?

If private views could more prevail,
Than ardour, for the public weal,
Then had his native, martial heat,
In arms seduc'd him to be great.

But godlike virtue, more inclin'd
To save, than to destroy,
Deems it superior joy,
To lead in chains of peace the mind.

With song, ye Britons, lead the day!
  Sing! sing the morn, that gave him breath,
Whose virtues never shall decay,
  No, never, never taste of death.

Chorus

When tombs and trophies shall be dust,
Fame shall preserve the great, and just.

For the King's Birthday 1732

Let there be light!
Such was at once the word and work of Heav'n,
  When from the void of universal night
  Free Nature sprang to the Creator's sight,
And day to glad the new-born world was giv'n.

Succeeding days to ages roll'd
And ev'ry age some wonder told:
At length arose this glorious morn!
  When, to extend his bounteous pow'r,
  High Heav'n announc'd this instant hour
The best of monarchs shall be born!

  Born to protect and bless the land!
And while the laws his people form,
His sceptre glories to confirm
  Their wishes are his sole command.

The word that form'd the world
  In vain did make mankind;
Unless, his passions to restrain,
  Almighty wisdom had design'd
Sometimes a William, or a George should reign.
Yet farther, Britons, cast your eyes,
Behold a long succession rise
Of future fair felicities.

  Around the royal table spread,
See how the beauteous branches shine!
  Sprung from the fertile genial bed
Of glorious George and Caroline.

  While Heav'n with bounteous hand
Has so enrich'd her store;
  When shall this promis'd land
In royal heirs be poor?
  All we can further ask, or Heav'n bestow,
  Is, that we long this happiness may know.

  While o'er our vanquish'd hearts alone
Our peaceful prince would greatly reign
  He bids obedience to his throne,
And haughty Britain hugs her chain.

  Her jealous sons, in George secure,
A happier state than freedom boast;
  For while his kind commands allure,
Freedom in hearts resign'd is lost.

  Sing, joyous Britons, sing
The glorious natal day,
  That gave, with such a king,
So great, so mild a sway.

Chorus

His realms around
Diffuse the sound!
From ports to fleets the jovial cannon play,
'Till ev'ry peaceful shore
Receives the rolling roar,
And joins the joy that crowns the day.

[7]
William Whitehead
(1715–1785)

Although William Whitehead was poet laureate for 28 years, a period in office exceeded only by Tennyson, Masefield, and Southey, his name lives on largely because he accepted the laureateship after it had been turned down by Thomas Gray, already famous for the *Elegy in a Country Churchyard* (1750).

When Colley Cibber died, aged 86, on 11 December 1757, the lord chamberlain, the duke of Devonshire, was determined Gray should be the next laureate. He was even willing to suspend the obligation to produce new year and birthday odes if the poet would accept. But Gray was adamant, as he made quite clear in his letter of refusal (see below). So the laurel went to Whitehead, who was glad to take it; unfortunately, he was nothing like famous enough to be excused the odes.

Whitehead had been born in Cambridge in February 1715, the second son of a baker. At the age of 14, thanks to the influence of a local dignitary who later became high steward of the university, he was sent to Winchester College. In 1733, two years after his father's death, he was lucky enough to win a small prize in a poetry competition sponsored by the earl of Peterborough, who was visiting the school with the poet Alexander Pope. As a result, Pope invited the young scholar to make a Latin translation of the first of the four epistles of his *Essay on Man*, which had just started to appear. No doubt, it proved a labour of love, for Whitehead remained a disciple of Pope all his life, although he never succeeded in matching the great man's wit.

Because of his humble background, Whitehead failed to secure a place at New College, Oxford, then as now, the preferred destination of most Wykehamists. Instead, he had to be content with Clare Hall, Cambridge, which he entered in 1735 with the aid of a minor scholarship designed to help the children of local tradesmen. Here he made the best of the opportunities that were now open to him. Among his friends was Charles Townshend (1725–67), famous in later life for taxing imports of tea into America, one of the factors that led to the revolutionary war with Britain. Whitehead addressed two of his early poems to him. Other youthful publications included a piece in celebration of the marriage of the prince of Wales in 1736, which he followed two years later with another in praise of the royal couple's first child, who later became George III. In June 1742 Whitehead's academic efforts were crowned with success, and he was elected a fellow of Clare, two months after his mother's death.

This college post lasted, however, for only a few years, for in 1745 the earl of Jersey engaged him as private tutor to his 10-year-old son, Lord Villiers, and Whitehead left Cambridge to live in London at the earl's home. As this appointment made him more or less independent, he was able to resign his fellowship; to have remained a fellow he would have had to take holy orders, something he was not prepared to do.

As a boy at Winchester, Whitehead had scored a number of successes performing in school plays. So when he settled in London, his thoughts turned once again to the theatre, though this time the attraction lay in writing rather than in acting. In April 1750 David Garrick, the famous actor-manager, staged a successful production at Drury Lane of Whitehead's first drama, a tragedy called *The Roman Father*. This was followed four years later by a second tragedy, *Creusa, Queen of Athens*. The second play, which was adapted from Euripedes, was highly praised by Horace Walpole ('the only new tragedy that I ever saw and really liked').

A couple of months later Whitehead set off with Lord Villiers and Lord Nuneham, a new pupil, on a long tour of the continent. Nuneham's father was the earl of Harcourt and had been acting as governor to the prince of Wales, afterwards George III, since 1751. Such grand tours, as they were called, were the accepted way for young men of good position to finish their education; and we can be sure Whitehead did everything to interest his charges in the language, arts, and history of the different countries they visited.

His reports must have pleased the two noble families back home: in 1755 word reached him in Italy of a new appointment. He had been made secretary and registrar of the Order of the Bath, which George I had established in 1725. This piece of good fortune he owed to Lord Villiers's mother, Lady Jersey, who had persuaded the duke of Newcastle, controller of all government patronage, to make the award. Whitehead and his party returned to England in the autumn of 1756, and for the next 23 years he lodged with the Jerseys or the Harcourts, having become a firm friend of both families. Early in 1757 he published the poems that he had written while he was abroad.

After Cibber's death in December 1757, the duke of Devonshire made his approach to Thomas Gray through an intermediary. This was the Rev. William Mason, a friend of the poet and a former tutor of the duke's younger brother, Lord John Cavendish, another friend of Gray. Ironically enough, Mason, a competent poet, had had hopes of the appointment. But the duke decided that the laureateship was unsuitable for a clergyman, and passed him over; he was soon made a king's chaplain, however, which must have helped to soften the blow. Gray himself was very explicit about his reasons for rejecting the laureateship. To Mason he wrote:

> Though I very well know the bland emollient saponaceous qualities both of sack and silver, yet if any great man would say to me, 'I make you rat-catcher to his Majesty, with a salary of £300 a year and two butts of the best Malaga; and though it has been usual to catch a mouse or two, for form's sake, in public once a year, yet to you, sir, we shall not stand upon these things,' I cannot say that I should jump at it; nay, if they would drop the very name of the office, and call me Sinecure to the King's Majesty, I should still feel a little awkward, and think everybody I saw smelt a rat about me.

War with France—the so-called Seven Years War, which involved simultaneous fighting in America and India as well as in Europe—had broken out in 1756. As usual with Britain in the early stages of a war, things had not gone well. The new laureate, however, was genuinely determined to play his part, and made a passionate appeal in his *Verses to the People of England* (1758) for the nation to rally behind its leaders. His willingness to put aside party differences, when he owed both his position and his pension to the court, added a refreshing new dimension to the responsibilities of his office, and is therefore much to Whitehead's credit.

The laureate's first official ode, for George II's 75th birthday, duly appeared in November that year. In a laudable attempt to try something different, he traced in verse the king's ancestry right back to one Ottoberto, who flourished in northern Italy 'about the year 963'. The only person prepared to quarrel with this was Edward Gibbon, the future historian. But he was only 21, so one assumes the author found it easy to ignore his strictures.

Throughout 28 eventful years of office—they included the whole war with America, which led to the birth of the United States—Whitehead regularly supplied his required quota of odes, suffering occasional attacks from satirists with characteristic forbearance and good humour. His interest in the theatre continued unabated. In 1762 his comedy, *The School for Lovers*, was produced at Drury Lane, meeting with enough success for Garrick to make him one of his readers, helping the management assess works submitted by hopeful dramatists. The post was not without its hazards. In 1767, for instance, Whitehead argued for rejecting Oliver Goldsmith's very first play, a comedy entitled *The Good Natur'd Man.* A tremendous set-to followed, involving Edmund Burke and Sir Joshua Reynolds, as well as Garrick, Whitehead, and the author; but the play was turned down. The laureate's last piece of work for the stage was a farce called *The Trip to Scotland.*

In August 1769 his old friend and patron the earl of Jersey died, and Whitehead, who never married, moved into London lodgings of his own. When he died on 14 April 1785, his papers included a copy of what is perhaps his most entertaining poem, *A Pathetic Apology for all Laureates, past, present, and to come.* It had circulated among his friends, but was not published until William Mason issued a memoir of his life in 1788.

For the New Year 1761

This was Whitehead's first ode to the new king, George III, who came to the throne on 25 October 1760. Its main theme, the vital importance to Britain of a strong navy, must have delighted the elder Pitt, then virtually prime minister, a vigorous exponent of the use of sea power in the Seven Years War (1756–63) with France, Austria, Sweden, and Russia. Outside Europe, where Britain was allied to Prussia (led by Frederick the Great), the main campaigns took place against the French in India and North America—where, says Whitehead, 'Canada is ours'—and effectively laid the foundations of the British empire. At Minden, in Westphalia, the Anglo-Prussian army scored a spectacular victory over the French.

Still must the Muse, indignant, hear
  The clanging trump, the rattling car,
And usher in each opening year
  With groans of death, and sounds of war?
O'er bleeding millions, realms opprest,
The tuneful mourner sinks distrest,
  Or breathes but notes of woe:
And cannot Gallia learn to melt,
Nor feel what Britain long has felt
  For her insulting foe?
Amidst her native rocks secure,
  Her floating bulwarks hovering round,
What can the sea-girt realm endure,
  What dread, through all her wat'ry bound?
Great queen of Ocean, she defies
All but the Power who rules the skies,
  And bids the storms engage;
Inferior foes are dash'd and lost,
As breaks the white wave on her coast
  Consum'd in idle rage.
For alien sorrows heaves her generous breast,
  She proffers peace to ease a rival's pain:
Her crowded ports, her fields in plenty drest,
  Bless the glad merchant, and th' industrious swain.

Do blooming youths in battle fall?
True to their fame the funeral urn we raise;
And thousands, at the glorious call,
Aspire to equal praise.

Thee, Glory, thee through climes unknown
Th' adventurous chief with zeal pursues;
And fame brings back from every zone
Fresh subjects for the British Muse.
Tremendous as th' ill-omen'd bird
To frighted France thy voice was heard
From Minden's echoing towers;
O'er Biscay's roar thy voice prevail'd;
And at thy word the rocks we scal'd,
And Canada is ours.
O potent queen of every breast
Which aims at praise by virtuous deeds,
Where'er thy influence shines confest
The hero acts, th' event succeeds.
But ah! must Glory only bear,
Bellona-like, the vengeful spear?
To fill her mighty mind
Must bulwarks fall, and cities flame,
And is her amplest field of fame
The miseries of mankind?
On ruins pil'd, on ruins must she rise,
And lend her rays to gild her fatal throne?
Must the mild Power who melts in vernal skies,
By thunders only make his godhead known?
No, be the omen far away;
From yonder pregnant cloud a kinder gleam,
Though faintly struggling into day,
Portends a happier theme!—

—And who is he, of regal mien,
Reclin'd on Albion's golden fleece,
Whose polish'd brow and eye serene
Proclaim him elder-born of peace?

Another George!—Ye winds convey
Th' auspicious name from pole to pole!
Thames, catch the sound, and tell the subject sea
Beneath whose sway its waters roll,
The hoary monarch of the deep,
Who sooth'd its murmurs with a father's care,
Doth now eternal sabbath keep,
And leaves his trident to his blooming heir.
O, if the Muse aright divine,
Fair Peace shall bless his opening reign,
And through its splendid progress shine,
With every art to grace her train.
The wreaths, so late by glory won,
Shall weave their foliage round his throne,
Till kings, abash'd, shall tremble to be foes,
And Albion's dreaded strength secure the world's
repose.

For the New Year 1777

Although the American Revolution began in 1775 (to be followed by six years of fighting), the Declaration of Independence was not signed until 4 July 1776. Its ringing phrases did not fall entirely upon deaf ears in Britain, as Whitehead implies. Many liberal-minded Englishmen, notably the M.P. Edmund Burke ('Deny them this participation of freedom, and you break that sole bond, which originally made, and must still preserve the unity of the empire') did not attempt to conceal their sympathy with the colonists. Some even hoped that a rebel victory would help to bring an end to George III's personal rule.

Again imperial Winter's sway
Bids the earth and air obey;
Throws o'er yon hostile lakes his icy bar,
And, for a while, suspends the rage of war.

O may it ne'er revive!—Ye wise,
Ye just, ye virtuous, and ye brave,
Leave fell contention to the sons of vice,
And join your powers to save!

Enough of slaughter have ye known,
Ye wayward children of a distant clime,
For you we heave the kindred groan,
We pity your misfortune, and your crime.
Stop, parricides, the blow,
O find another foe!
And hear a parent's dear request,
Who longs to clasp you to her yielding breast.

What change would ye require? What form
Ideal floats in fancy's sky?
Ye fond enthusiasts break the charm,
And let cool reason clear the mental eye.
On Britain's well-mix'd state alone,
True Liberty has fix'd her throne,
Where law, not man, an equal rule maintains:
Can freedom e'er be found where many a tyrant reigns?

United, let us all those blessings find,
The God of Nature meant mankind,
Whate'er of error, ill redrest;
Whate'er of passion, ill represt;
Whate'er the wicked have conceiv'd,
And folly's heedless sons believ'd,
Let all lie buried in oblivion's flood,
And our great cement be—the public good.

A Pathetic Apology for all Laureates, past, present, and to come

This good-humoured defence of the laureateship was published only after Whitehead's death. It appeared in 1788 in an edition of his collected works, but had previously been circulated 'for the amusement of a few friends'.

Ye silly dogs, whose half-year lays
Attend like satellites on Bays;
And still, with added lumber, load
Each birthday and each new year ode,
Why will ye *strive* to be *severe*?
In pity to yourselves forbear;
Nor let the sneering public see,
What numbers write far worse than he.

His muse, *oblig'd* by sack and pension,
Without a subject, or invention—
Must certain words in order set,
As innocent as a gazette;
Must some half-meaning half disguise,
And utter neither truth nor lies.
But why will *you*, ye volunteers
In nonsense, tease us with your jeers,
Who *might* with dulness and her crew
Securely slumber? Why will *you*
Sport your dim orbs amidst her fogs?
You're not *oblig'd*—ye silly dogs!

When Jove, as ancient fables sing,
Made of a senseless log a King,
The frogs at first, their doubts exprest;
But soon leap'd up, and smok'd the jest.

While every tadpole of the lake
Lay quiet, tho' they felt it quake,
They knew their nature's due degree,
Themselves scarce more alive than he;
They knew they could not croak like frogs.
—Why will *you* try?—ye silly dogs!

When the poor barber felt askance,
The thunder of a Quixote's lance,
For merely bearing on his head,
Th' expressive emblem of his trade,
The barber was a harmless log,
The hero was a silly dog—
What trivial things are cause of quarrel!
Mambrino's helmet, or the laurel,
Alike distract an idiot's brain,
'Unreal mockeries!' shadowy pain!

Each Laureat (if kind heav'n dispense
Some little gleam of common sense)
Blest with *one hundred pounds* per ann.
And that too taxed and but ill-paid,
With caution frames his frugal plan,
Nor apes his brethren of the trade.
He never will to garrets rise
For inspiration from the skies;
And pluck, as Hotspur would have done,
'Bright honour, from the pale-faced moon';
He never will to cellars venture,
To drag up glory from the centre;
But calmly steer his course between
Th' aerial and infernal scene;
—*One hundred pounds!* a golden mean!

Nor need *he* ask a printer's pains
To fix the type, and share the gains:
Each morning paper is so kind
To give his works to every wind.

Each evening post and magazine,
Gratis adopts the *lay serene.*
On their frail barks his praise or blame
Floats for an hour, and sinks with them;
Sure without envy you might see,
Such floundering immortality.
Why will ye then, amidst the bogs,
Thrust in *your* oar?—ye silly dogs!

He ne'er desires his stated loan,
(I honestly can speak for one)
Should meet in print the public eye;
Content with Boyce's harmony,
Who throws, on many a worthless lay,
His music and his powers away.

Are *you* not charm'd, when, at Vauxhall,
Or Marybone, the Syrens squall
Your oft-repeated madrigals,
Your Nancys of the hills or vales,
While tip-toe misses and their beaux
Catch the dear sounds in triple rows,
And whisper, as their happiness,
They know the author of the piece?
This vanity, my gentle brothers,
You feel; forgive it then in others,
At least in one you call a dunce,
The Laureat's odes are sung but once,
And then not heard—while your renown
For half a season stuns the town—
Nay, on brown paper, fairly spread,
With wooden print to grace its head,
Each barber pastes you on his wall;
Each cobbler chants you in his stall,
And Dolly, from her master's shop,
Encores you, as she twirls her mop.

Then 'ponder well, ye parents dear'
Of works, which live a whole half year;
And with a tender eye survey
The frailer offspring of a day,
Whose glories wither e'er they bloom,
Whose very cradle is their tomb:
Have ye no bowels, cruel men!
You who may grasp, or quit the pen,
May chuse your subject, nay, your time,
When genius prompts to sport in rhime;
Dependant on yourselves alone,
To be immortal, or unknown:
Does not compassion touch your breast
For brethren to the service prest?
To laureats is no pity due,
Incumber'd with a thousand clogs?
I'm very sure they *pity* you,
—Ye silliest of all silly dogs.

[8]
Thomas Warton
(1728–1790)

Sir John Betjeman, the present poet laureate, has won considerable fame for reminding us of the significance of long-forgotten Victorian architects and designers. How much more should we value the work of Thomas Warton, the 18th-century scholar and laureate, whose love of the past did so much to revive interest in medieval life and literature, and made him one of the great forerunners of the Romantic movement.

Born on 9 January 1728 at Basingstoke, Hampshire, Warton came from a markedly literary family. His father, Thomas, who was a friend of Alexander Pope, wrote verse and was professor of poetry at Oxford from 1718 to 1728. He had become vicar of Basingstoke in 1723, a job he combined with the headmastership of the local grammar school. (One of his pupils was Gilbert White, the future naturalist of Selborne.) Thomas's elder brother Joseph, who later became headmaster of Winchester College, also turned out to be a poet.

Young Thomas, who began writing verse before he was ten, was educated at home until he was 16. Then, in March 1744, he went up to Trinity College, Oxford, one of the Jacobite strongholds in a university well known for supporting the Stuart cause, and notorious for its idleness and dissipation. He graduated B.A. in 1747 (two years after his father's death), became a clergyman, and started work as a college tutor. That same year, too, he published *The Pleasures of Melancholy*, a blank-verse poem that drew its inspiration from his two favourite poets, Edmund Spenser and John Milton. Written during his 17th year, it showed how early he had learned to appreciate the importance of 16th- and 17th-century poetry (not then at all fashionable).

Warton also developed an abiding enthusiasm for medieval

architecture, especially for old castles, churches, and monasteries, which he studied during his vacations. Polite society, though, felt that such things were barbarous and uncouth. They labelled them Gothic, preferring, if possible, to replace them with new buildings that were more strictly 'classical'. By his writings and by his example, Warton helped to rekindle interest in the middle ages. This in turn made Gothic architecture fashionable—allied to a growing interest in natural landscape—and so helped to encourage a parallel liking for the romantic in literature. Warton was thus an influential forerunner of the whole Romantic movement.

Warton's own commitment to Gothic had been made abundantly clear in his *Triumph of Isis* (1749), an heroic poem written in praise of Oxford, with particular emphasis on its architectural attractions. The poem was a reply to William Mason's *Isis*, a denunciation of the university's Stuart leanings, which had been published in 1746, the year after Bonnie Prince Charlie's abortive rising in Scotland.

Warton acted as a spur to other, like-minded, university folk, who were persuaded by his example to exercise their literary skills. When he was 19, he initiated a scheme in the bachelors' common room at Trinity for the annual election of a poet laureate, whose duties were to sing the praises of some 'lady patroness'. He himself held the post for two years. He also became an active contributor to a university magazine and to various collections of poetry. In fact, he was rapidly developing into an Oxford character, just as happy drinking in a pothouse with the local watermen as he was carousing in college. Out of term, he spent much of his time relaxing at Winchester College, where he became a great favourite. He was famous for ghosting the boys' exercises (with 'errors' built-in); and the headmaster, on the prowl one day for illicit cooking, actually surprised his brother, who was one of the culprits, hiding in a dark corner.

But unlike so many 18th-century dons (he became a fellow of Trinity in 1751), Warton was able to channel his enthusiasm, his energy and his academic leisure into an enormous amount of original reading. The first proof of his wide scholarship appeared in his *Observations on the Faery Queen of Spenser* (1754), published when he was only 26.

Dr Johnson, who was then completing his great *Dictionary*, warmly approved of the book. He was particularly impressed by the way the author had introduced many illustrative parallels from other writers, a special feature of his dictionary. As a result, the two men became firm friends, although they met only infrequently. It was largely thanks to Warton that Johnson secured his M.A. the following February, just in time to use it on the title page of his dictionary.

When he was 29, Thomas Warton was elected professor of poetry, an appointment he held for ten years. In those days the lectures were given in Latin and covered only classical poetry. The position was a demanding one, leaving little time for English studies. But he was not the sort of man to take life or work too seriously. In 1760 he brought out *A Companion to the Guide and a Guide to the Companion*, a satire on Oxford guidebooks and antiquarian studies; in it he included information about coffee-houses and inns, billiard tables and skittle-alleys.

This book appeared anonymously, as did *The Oxford Sausage* (1764), his anthology of university poetry and humour, which continued to entertain readers for almost 60 years. At the end of his professorship, he took his Bachelor of Divinity degree. Four years later in 1771, he became vicar of Kiddington, a village near Oxford, and was elected a fellow of the Society of Antiquaries in London. This may well have encouraged him to write the history of the parish, which he published a couple of years later. Once again, he was an innovator, hoping his example would encourage others to write histories of the different English counties.

But these were minor activities. Since ceasing to be professor of poetry, he had been absorbed in a monumental undertaking, *The History of English Poetry*. The first book appeared in 1774, with two further volumes in 1778 and 1781. The third volume ended with the Elizabethan age, but the series itself, which he had planned should finish with Pope, was never completed. The history had a mixed reception, largely because it was an inaugural work of scholarship produced at a time when readers were not really prepared for an orderly historical approach. Earlier attempts in this field had amounted to little more than collections of anecdotes of the lives of poets arranged without any real perspective. Indeed, one of Warton's greatest gifts was his ability to assess the subject matter as an historian, while resisting the temptation to show off as a critic. The amount of labour involved was prodigious—old books and manuscripts were scattered in libraries and collections all over the country, and no proper catalogues existed.

During much of this time Warton's friendship with Johnson had cooled. But relations improved after the publication of the second volume of the *History*, and in 1782 Warton became a member of the most influential literary society in London, the Literary Club, which had been started in 1764 by Sir Joshua Reynolds and Dr Johnson.

William Whitehead died on 14 April 1785, and 12 days later the 57-year-old Warton took his place. Such a distinguished Oxford scholar and versatile poet—he had just been elected professor of ancient history, and his elegant edition of Milton's minor poems was due out in a few months—must have seemed the ideal choice, a man destined to bring fresh lustre to the laureateship.

His first official offering, an ode for the king's birthday, on 4 June, was inevitably a rushed job, and retribution followed swiftly. Within a few weeks appeared *Probationary Odes for the Laureateship*, an ingenious fabrication by a group of lively satirists, supporters of Charles James Fox, whose Whig coalition had been defeated at the end of 1784 by young William Pitt, who became prime minister. The book contained 22 odes, each of which, it was asserted, had been recited at a competition held at the lord chamberlain's office to choose the new poet laureate. Twenty-one of the poems were ludicrous parodies, including one ascribed to Warton's brother Joseph. The final piece, needless to say, was Warton's own birthday ode. Nobody enjoyed the joke more than he did.

Over the next three years Warton supplied his biannual quota of work. But in November 1788 he was suddenly confronted by a situation no other laureate had ever had to face—his sovereign went mad. (In recent years, however, it has been suggested that the king suffered from porphyria, an hereditary illness with symptoms similar to those of insanity.) No ode was needed for the following

January; but by April George III had quite recovered, which posed problems for the June birthday ode. Warton's solution was to tackle the matter obliquely, neatly comparing the king's recent illness to a summer storm briefly darkening the landscape before 'the reddening Sun regains his golden sway'.

As it happened, this was the last of his odes to be performed, for no court ceremony was held on new year's day 1790 either. Four months later Warton had a severe stroke while sitting in the common-room at Trinity. He died the next day, and was buried in the college ante-chapel. His ode for the next royal birthday was already completed.

For the King's Birthday 1787

In this roll-call of some of the major English poets Warton follows tradition in suggesting that both Chaucer and Spenser were his predecessors in office. Naturally enough, he is generous in his recognition of Spenser, whose Faery Queen *was the subject of one of his best-known books. But the absurd assertion that the monarchs these poets served must yield in might to George III is pure anti-climax; it was at once ridiculed by 'Peter Pindar' (John Wolcot), author of various satirical poems about the king.*

The noblest Bards of Albion's choir
Have struck of old this festal lyre.
Ere Science, struggling oft in vain,
Had dar'd to break her Gothic chain,
Victorious Edward gave the vernal bough
Of Britain's bay to bloom on Chaucer's brow:
Fir'd with the gift, he chang'd to sounds sublime
His Norman minstrelsy's discordant chime;
In tones majestic hence he told
The banquet of Cambuscan bold;

And oft he sung (howe'er the rhyme
Has moulder'd to the touch of time)
His martial master's knightly board,
And Arthur's ancient rites restor'd;
The prince in sable steel that sternly frown'd,
And Gallia's captive king, and Cressy's wreath renown'd.

Won from the shepherd's simple meed,
The whispers wild of Mulla's reed,
Sage Spenser wak'd his lofty lay
To grace Eliza's golden sway:
O'er the proud theme new lustre to diffuse,
He chose the gorgeous allegoric Muse,
And call'd to life old Uther's elfin tale,
And rov'd thro' many a necromantic vale,
Portraying chiefs that knew to tame
The goblin's ire, the dragon's flame,
To pierce the dark enchanted hall,
Where Virtue sate in lonely thrall.
From fabling Fancy's inmost store
A rich romantic robe he bore;
A veil with visionary trappings hung,
And o'er his virgin-queen the fairy texture flung.

At length the matchless Dryden came,
To light the Muses' clearer flame;
To lofty numbers grace to lend,
And strength with melody to blend;
To triumph in the bold career of song,
And roll th' unwearied energy along.
Does the mean incense of promiscuous praise,
Does servile fear, disgrace his regal bays?
I spurn his panegyric strings,
His partial homage, tun'd to kings!
Be mine, to catch his manlier chord,
That paints th' impassioned Persian lord,

By glory fir'd, to pity su'd,
Rous'd to revenge, by love subdu'd;
And still, with transport new, the strains to trace,
That chant the Theban pair, and Tancred's deadly vase.

Had these blest Bards been call'd, to pay
The vows of this auspicious day,
Each had confess'd a fairer throne,
A mightier sovereign than his own!
Chaucer had made his hero-monarch yield
The martial fame of Cressy's well-fought field
To peaceful prowess, and the conquests calm,
That braid the sceptre with the patriot's palm:
His chaplets of fantastic bloom,
His colourings, warm from Fiction's loom,
Spenser had cast in scorn away,
And deck'd with truth alone the lay;
All real here, the bard had seen
The glories of his pictur'd Queen!
The tuneful Dryden had not flatter'd here,
His lyre had blameless been, his tribute all sincere.

For the King's Birthday 1789

In November 1788 George III was stricken with his first apparent attack of insanity, which lasted about four months. As a result Warton published no ode on 1 January 1789 or indeed on the following new year's day; but he then faced the problem of dealing with the king's health in his next birthday ode. These verses show how discreetly he handled the matter.

As when the demon of the summer storm
Walks forth the noontide landscape to deform,
Dark grows the vale, and dark the distant grove,
And thick the bolts of angry Jove
Athwart the wat'ry welkin glide,
And streams the aerial torrent far and wide:

If by short fits the struggling ray
Should dart a momentary day,
Th' illumin'd mountain glows awhile,
By faint degrees the radiant glance
Purples th' horizon's pale expanse,
And gilds the gloom with hasty smile:
Ah! fickle smile, too swiftly past!
Again resounds the sweeping blast,
With hoarser din the demon howls;
Again the blackening concave scowls;
Sudden the shades of the meridian night
Yield to the triumph of rekindling light;
The reddening Sun regains his golden sway;
And Nature stands revealed in all her bright array.

Such was the changeful conflict that possess'd
With trembling tumult every British breast,
When Albion, towering in the van sublime
Of Glory's march, from clime to clime
Envied, belov'd, rever'd, renown'd,
Her brows with every blissful chaplet bound,
When, in her mid career of state,
She felt her monarch's awful fate!
Till Mercy from th' Almighty throne
Look'd down on man, and waving wide
Her wreath that, in the rainbow dyed,
With hues of soften'd lustre shone,
And bending from her sapphire cloud
O'er regal grief benignant bow'd;
To transport turn'd a people's fears,
And stay'd a people's tide of tears:
Bade this blest dawn with beams auspicious spring,
With hope serene, with healing on its wing;
And gave a sovereign o'er a grateful land
Again with vigorous grasp to stretch the scepter'd hand.

O favour'd king, what rapture more refin'd,
What mightier joy can fill the human mind,
Than what monarch's conscious bosom feels,
At whose dread throne a nation kneels,
And hails its father, friend, and lord,
To life's career, to partiot sway restor'd;
And bids the loud responsive voice
Of union all around rejoice?
For thus to thee when Britons bow,
Warm and spontaneous from the heart,
As late their tears, their transports start,
And nature dictates duty's vow.
To thee, recall'd to sacred health,
Did the proud city's lavish wealth,
Did crowded streets alone display
The long-drawn blaze, the festal ray?
Meek Poverty her scanty cottage grac'd,
And flung her gleam across the lonely waste!
Th' exulting isle in one wide triumph strove,
One social sacrifice of reverential love!

Such pure unprompted praise do kingdoms pay,
Such willing zeal, to thrones of lawless sway?
Ah! how unlike the vain, the venal lore,
To Latian rulers dealt of yore,
O'er guilty pomp and hated power
When stream'd the sparkling panegyric shower;
And slaves, to sovereigns unendear'd,
Their pageant trophies coldly rear'd!
For are the charities, that blend
Monarch with man, to tyrants known?
The tender ties, that to the throne
A mild domestic glory lend,
Of wedded love the league sincere,
The virtuous consort's faithful tear?
Nor this the verse, that flattery brings,
Nor here I strike a Siren's strings;

Here kindling with her country's warmth, the Muse
Her country's proud triumphant theme pursues;
E'en needless here the tribute of her lay!
Albion the garland gives on this distinguish'd day.

For the King's Birthday 1790

This ode, the last from Warton's pen, was found among his papers after his death and published later that year. In singing the topographical attractions of Britain's fashionable health spas and watering places, he must have drawn on his own experience as a frequent traveller up and down the country. The final stanza, which refers to Weymouth, Dorset, was highly topical. George III and Queen Charlotte had spent several weeks there the previous summer in the hope of hastening the king's recovery from his recent attack of insanity. The diarist Fanny Burney, the second keeper of robes to Queen Charlotte, had noted that a bathing machine 'follows the Royal one into the sea, filled with fiddlers, who play God save the King, *as his Majesty takes his plunge!'*

Within what fountain's craggy cell
Delights the goddess Health to dwell,
Where from the rigid roof distills
Her richest stream in steely rills?
What mineral gems intwine her humid locks?
Lo! sparkling high from potent springs
To Britain's sons her cup she brings!
Romantic Matlock! are thy tufted rocks,
Thy fring'd declivities, the dim retreat
Where the coy nymph has fix'd her favourite seat,
And hears, reclin'd along the thundering shore,
Indignant Darwent's desultory tide
His rugged channel rudely chide,
Darwent, whose shaggy wreath is stain'd with Danish gore?

Or does she dress her naiad cave
With coral spoils from Neptune's wave,
And hold short revels with the train
Of nymphs that tread the neighbouring main,
And from the cliffs of Avon's cavern'd side
Temper the balmy beverage pure,
That, fraught with drops of precious cure,
Brings back to trembling hope the drooping bride,
That in the virgin's cheek renews the rose,
And wraps the eye of pain in quick repose?
While oft she climbs the mountain's shelving steeps,
And calls her votaries wan to catch the gale,
That breathes o'er Ashton's elmy vale,
And from the Cambrian hills the billowy Severn sweeps!

Or broods the nymph with watchful wing
O'er ancient Badon's mystic spring,
And speeds from its sulphureous source
The steamy torrent's secret course,
And fans th' eternal sparks of hidden fire,
In deep unfathom'd beds below
By Bladud's magic taught to glow,
Bladud, high theme of Fancy's gothic lyre?
Or opes the healing power her chosen fount
In the rich veins of Malvern's ample mount,
From whose tall ridge the noontide wanderer views
Pomona's purple realm, in April's pride,
Its blaze of bloom expanding wide,
And waving groves array'd in Flora's fairest hues?

Haunts she the scene, where Nature low'rs
O'er Buxton's heath in lingering show'rs?
Or loves she more, with sandal fleet
In matin dance the nymphs to meet,
That on the flowery marge of Chelder play?
Who, boastful of the stately train,
That deign'd to grace his simple plain,

Late with new pride along his reedy way
Bore to Sabrina wreaths of brighter hue,
And mark'd his pastoral urn with emblems new.
Howe'er these streams ambrosial may detain
Thy steps, O genial Health, yet not alone
   Thy gifts the naiad sisters own;
Thine too the briny flood, and Ocean's hoar domain.

   And lo, amid the watery roar
In Thetis' car she skims the shore,
   Where Portland's brows, embattled high
   With rocks, in rugged majesty
Frown o'er the billows, and the storm restrain,
   She beckons Britain's scepter'd pair
   Her treasures of the deep to share!
Hail then, on this glad morn, the mighty main!
Which leads the boon divine of lengthen'd days
To those who wear the noblest regal bays:
That mighty main, which on its conscious tide
Their boundless commerce pours on every clime,
   Their dauntless banner bears sublime;
And wafts their pomp of war, and spreads their thunder wide!

[9]
Henry Pye
(1745–1813)

In the 300-year-old history of the laureateship nothing is more inexplicable than Henry James Pye's decision to exchange the time-honoured butt of Canary wine—a custom dating from the pre-laureate days of Ben Jonson—for an annual payment of £27. It is hard to believe that such a notion could have come from Pye himself, an officer in the militia, a county magistrate, and a former member of the House of Commons; but no documents relating to the case survive, so it remains a complete mystery. Understandably, Robert Southey, his immediate successor, called it a wicked decision.

Pye, the last of the 18th-century laureates, was born at Faringdon, Berkshire, on 20 February 1745, the eldest son of Henry Pye. His father became one of the M.P.s for Berkshire the following year, and retained his seat until his death 20 years later. After being educated at home, young Pye went to Magdalen College, Oxford, as a commoner in 1762. This was also the year he published his first poem, an ode on the birth of the prince of Wales (later George IV), which appeared in a collection of Oxford verse.

Just before Pye graduated in 1766, his father died, leaving him the family estates at Faringdon—together with debts amounting to £50,000. To make matters worse, the family mansion burnt down soon after, which increased his liabilities because he decided to rebuild. He still managed to publish poetry, however, and the following year, at the age of 21, he married Mary Hook, a colonel's daughter. She bore him two daughters, and even wrote a farce, *The Capricious Lady*, which was staged at Drury Lane theatre in May 1771.

After his marriage, Pye joined the Berkshire militia, became a county magistrate, and settled down to write verse. Over the years he produced an extensive number of poems and translations, including a version of Frederick the Great's *Art of War* (1778), which the Prussian king, who was eager to rank as a distinguished French author, had written in French. As well as military matters, open-air sports seem to have been a favourite occupation of Pye's, an interest he turned to good use in 1784, when he published a long poem entitled *Shooting*. He was also quick to celebrate the advent of ballooning, with his poem *Aeraphonon*. This appeared in 1784, when Vincent Lunardi, secretary to the Neapolitan ambassador, became the first person in England to make an ascent, which he did in the presence of the prince of Wales and an enormous crowd.

The general election that year proved to be significant. William Pitt, prime minister at 24 and passionate advocate of free trade and parliamentary reform, was returned with a large majority. His victory was an obvious expression of the country's deep-rooted desire for constitutional, economic, and social improvement, although the French Revolution (1789) and the years of war that followed it put paid all too soon to most of these hopes. Among the ten members for Berkshire returned that year was Henry Pye. But unlike his father before him, he held the seat for only a few years. In 1790 he failed to secure re-election, and retired from the political scene.

For Pye, however, a new chapter was about to begin. On 21 May Thomas Warton, the poet laureate, died of a stroke, just two weeks before George III's 52nd birthday; and on 28 July, the lucky Pye succeeded him, a reward for his loyal support of Pitt. It was a post he was to hold for the next 23 years. As a poet, he brought little to the laureateship except a facility for churning out a series of mechanical odes, which he did with unfailing regularity until 1810, when George III became permanently insane, so freeing him from the obligation to produce public poems for the remaining three years of his life. But apart from a somewhat scornful satire, *Epistle to the Poet Laureate*, published soon after he took office, the opposition to Pye's appointment and to his subsequent publications was about as lukewarm as his own verses. One of his earliest odes was indeed ridiculed by George Steevens, a Shakespearean editor and friend of Dr Johnson, who focussed attention on Pye's rather stale poetic language. But the fun seems to have been goodnatured enough. When singing about the countryside, poets had long been addicted to such descriptive terms as the 'feathered choir' and the 'finny tribe'. The practice was more an expression of an interest in order and classification rather than affectation or laziness; but by the end of the century much of this phraseology had been emptied of meaning. So there was considerable delight when Steevens turned to 'Sing a song of sixpence', already an old rhyme, and asked: 'When the Pye was opened the birds began to sing; Was not that a dainty dish to set before the king?'.

Perhaps inspired by his wife's earlier example, and certainly following in the best traditions of the laureateship, Pye began to turn his attention to the theatre. In all, he wrote two tragedies and a comedy. But his most famous connection with the stage was of rather a different kind. In 1795 he was one of many who were completely taken in by the works of William Ireland, an 18-year-old forger of extraordinary boldness, whose handwritten fabrications included two 'Shakespeare' plays—*Henry II* and *Vortigern and Rowena*. Pye was persuaded to write a prologue for the latter, which Richard Sheridan had bought for performance at Drury Lane on 2 April 1796. Ireland's father, however, withdrew the prologue at the last minute because it was a shade too sceptical. For Pye this turned out to be a lucky decision—the first-night audience was not deceived and greeted the proceedings with shouts of laughter, and Ireland soon after made a full confession.

As an armchair strategist and student of military matters, Pye continued to show his worth. In 1795 he brought out a translation of the martial elegies of Tyrtaeus (an ancient Greek poet), which had once inspired Spartan soldiers to heroic feats in battle. Three years later he followed it up with *Naucratia—or Naval Dominion*, a versified account of sea warfare from its beginnings, which he dedicated to George III. According to Thomas Mathias in his satire *The Pursuits of Literature*, published in 1796, Pye's translation of Tyrtaeus was read aloud to five different militia regiments on parade; 'But before they were half finished, all the front ranks, and as many of the others as were within hearing or verse-shot, dropped their arms suddenly, and were *all found fast asleep*! Marquis Townshend, who never approved of the scheme, said, with his usual pleasantry, that the first of all poets observed that "Sleep is the brother of *Death*."' Alas, history does not record if any comparable experiments were carried out on board British men-o'-war.

If the wide range of subject-matter that Pye concerned himself with is anything to go by, few laureates have taken their duties more seriously. He was, for instance, among the first English poets to choose Alfred the Great as a fitting subject for an epic poem (1801)—but then the king was born at Wantage, only seven miles from Pye's country home. And he is certainly the only poet laureate to have published a book on the duties of a magistrate (1808), the direct result of his 40 years on the bench. (Curiously enough, in late Victorian times, Alfred Austin, one of his successors, also chose Alfred for a poetic drama; but being Austin, he thought no one else had ever thought of the idea before.) As further evidence of Pye's versatility, one should cite his *Comments on the Commentators of Shakespeare*. Self-appointed editors had been tampering with Shakespeare's text ever since Nicholas Rowe's edition of 1709 (p. 46). So it was hardly surprising that by the end of the 18th century reaction had set in against the restorers and in favour of texts that could be read without the distraction of editorial paraphernalia. Pye himself was wholly in favour of this move toward simplification. Referring to the iniquities of annotation, he remarked, by way of analogy, that dung was necessary for soil, and scaffolding for buildings; but who, he asked, when the work was finished, would make an ostentatious display of either?

In 1810, when Pye published his collected poems, his writing days were almost at an end. But although George III's final collapse into madness occurred that year and odes were therefore no longer performed in public, the laureate, dutiful as ever, continued to turn them out until his death, at Pinner, on 11 August 1813. He left two children by his first wife, who had died in 1796, and a son by his second wife, Martha, who he had married in 1801. As Sir Walter Scott later remarked, he was 'eminently respectable in everything but his poetry'.

For the New Year 1791

By 1790 the French Revolution was well under way, forcing radicals in England to decide where they stood with regard to political and social reform at home. In October 1790 Pitt's government, alarmed by increasing demands for parliamentary reform and by growing support for the idea of universal suffrage, suspended the Habeas Corpus Act. But Pye stood aloof, in this, his first ode, preferring to expatiate on the advantages of overseas trade and exploration. His references to Iberia (Spain) and Calpe (the ancient name for Gibraltar) would have reminded his readers of the great siege of 1779–83, when the Rock resisted strenuous Spanish efforts to seize it. Furthermore, Spain had only just agreed, in October 1790, to pay reparations for an attack on a small British settlement on the Pacific coast of Canada.

When from the bosom of the mine
The magnet first to light was thrown,
Fair Commerce hail'd the gift divine,
And, smiling, claim'd it for her own.
'My bark (she said) this gem shall guide,
Thro' paths of ocean yet untried,
While as my daring sons explore
Each rude inhospitable shore,
'Mid desert sands and ruthless skies,
New seats of industry shall rise.
And culture wide extend its genial reign,
Free as the ambient gale, and boundless as the main.'

But Tyranny soon learn'd to seize,
The art improving Science taught,
The white sail courts the distant breeze,
With horror and destruction fraught;
From the tall mast fell war unfurl'd
His banners to a new-found world;
Oppression, arm'd with giant pride,
And bigot Fury by her side;
Dire Desolation bath'd in blood,
Pale Avrice, and her harpy brood,
To each affrighted shore in thunder spoke,
And bow'd the wretched race to Slav'ry's iron yoke.

Not such the gentler views that urge
Britannia's sons to dare the surge;
Not such the gifts her Drake, her Raleigh bore
To the wild inmates of th' Atlantic shore,
Teaching each drear wood's pathless scene
The glories of their virgin queen.
Nor such her later chiefs, who try,
Impell'd by soft humanity,
The boist'rous wave, the rugged coast,
The burning zone, the polar frost,
That climes remote, and regions yet unknown,
May share a George's sway, and bless his patriot throne.

Warm Fancy, kindling with delight,
Anticipates the lapse of age,
And as she throws her eagle's flight
O'er time's yet undiscover'd page,
Vast continents, now dark with shade,
She sees in Verdure's robe array'd,
Sees o'er each island's fertile steep
That frequent studs the southern deep,
His fleecy charge the shepherd lead,
The harvest wave, the vintage bleed:
Sees Commerce, springs of guiltless wealth explore,
Where frowns the western world on Asia's neighbouring shore.

But, lo! across the blackening skies,
What swarthy demon wings his flight?
At once the transient landscape flies,
The splendid vision sets in night.
And see Britannia's awful form,
With breast undaunted, brave the storm:
Awful, as when her angry tide
O'erwhelm'd the wreck'd Armada's pride.
Awful, as when the avenging blow
Suspending o'er a prostrate foe,
She snatch'd in vict'ry's moment, prompt to save,
Iberia's sinking sons from Calpe's glowing wave.

Ere yet the tempest's mingled sound
Burst dreadful o'er the nations round,
What angel shape, in beaming radiance dight,
Pours through the severing clouds celestial light!
'Tis Peace—before her seraph eye
The fiends of devastation fly.
Auspicious, round our monarch's brow
She twines her olive's sacred bough;
This victory, she cries, is mine,
Not torn from war's terrific shrine!
Mine the pure trophies of the wise and good,
Unbought by scenes of woe, and undefil'd with blood.

For the King's Birthday 1794

By 4 June 1794, George III's 56th birthday, Britain had already been at war with France for 16 months. The previous year had seen the execution of Louis XVI (in January), the start of the reign of terror (June), the abolition of Christianity, and the execution of Marie-Antoinette (October). Between them, the crowned heads of Europe were now determined to crush the revolution and restore the French monarchy. But once again Pye remained extraordinarily detached from the great events of the day, even though British troops had been severely defeated in April 1794 in Flanders, where they had been sent to help Austrian forces attack northern France. The government, under William Pitt, who had begun the war convinced it would be short, now tightened its grip on those who sympathized with the revolution. Early in May, less than a month before Pye published his ode, Pitt suspended habeas corpus (this time for eight years) and banned all public meetings.

Rous'd from the gloom of transient death,
Reviving Nature's charms appear;
Mild zephyr wakes with balmy breath
The beauties of the youthful year,
The fleecy storm that froze the plain,
The winds that swept the billowy main,

The chilling blast, the icy show'r,
That oft obscur'd the vernal hour,
And half deform'd th' etherial grace
That bloom'd on Maia's lovely face,
Are gone—and o'er the fertile glade,
In manhood's riper form array'd,

Bright June appears, and from his bosom throws,
Blushing with hue divine, his own ambrosial rose.

Yet there are climes where winter hoar
  Despotic still usurps the plains,
Where the loud surges lash the shore,
  And dreary desolation reigns!—
While, as the shivering swain descries
The drifted mountains round him rise,
Through the dark mist and howling blast,
Full many a longing look is cast
To northern realms, whose happier skies detain
The lingering car of day, and check his golden rein.

Chide not his stay;—the roseate spring
Not always flies on halcyon wing;
Not always strains of joy and love
Steal sweetly through the trembling grove—
Reflecting Sol's refulgent beams,
The falchion oft terrific gleams;
And, louder than the wintr'y tempest's roar,
The battle's thunder shakes th' affrighted shore—
Chide not his stay—for, in the scenes,
  Where nature boasts her genial pride,
Where forests spread their leafy screens,
  And lucid streams the painted vales divide;
Beneath Europa's mildest clime
In glowing summer's verdant prime,
The frantic sons of Rapine tear
The golden wreath from Ceres' hair,

And trembling Industry, afraid
To turn the war-devoted glade,
Exposes wild to Famine's haggard eyes
Wastes where no hopes of future harvests rise,
While floating corses choke th' unpurpled flood,
And ev'ry dewy sod is stain'd with civic blood.

Vanish the horrid scene, and turn the eyes
To where Britannia's chalky cliffs arise.—
What though beneath her rougher air
A less luxuriant soil we share;
Though often o'er her brightest day
Sails the thick storm, and shrouds the solar ray,
No purple vintage though she boast,
No olive shade her ruder coast;
Yet here immortal Freedom reigns,
And law protects what labour gains;
And as her manly sons behold
The cultur'd farm, the teeming fold,
See Commerce spread to ev'ry gale
From every shore, her swelling sail;
Jocund, they raise the choral lay
To celebrate th' auspicious day,
By heaven selected from the laughing year,
Sacred to patriot worth, to patriot bosoms dear.

For the New Year 1806

With this new ode Pye strove valiantly to do justice to Nelson's victory at Trafalgar on 21 October 1805 over the French and Spanish fleets. When news of the battle reached London on 6 November, it was greeted with enormous relief; but there was little rejoicing, such was the grief at Nelson's death. As Robert Southey, Pye's successor, wrote in his Life of Nelson *(1813): 'An object of our admiration and affection, of our pride and of our hopes, was suddenly taken from us; and it seemed as if we had never, till then, known how deeply we loved and reverenced him.' Pye himself had some knowledge of the history of sea warfare—stanza two refers to his poem* Naucratia—or Naval Dominion *(1798). By Haffnia (a latinized version of Hagen, meaning harbour), the laureate refers to Copenhagen, where on 2 April 1801 Nelson had led a successful attack on the Danish fleet. The famous incident of the telescope and the blind eye occurred during that battle. 'Prore', in stanza five, is an archaic term for prow. In the ode Pye traces the course of recent events, including Nelson's pursuit of the French fleet across the Atlantic and back the previous summer. His poem appeared a week before Nelson's funeral at St Paul's.*

When ardent zeal for virtuous fame,
When virtuous honour's holy flame;
  Sit on the gen'rous warrior's sword,
Weak is the loudest lay the Muse can sing,
  His deeds of valour to record;
And weak the boldest flights of Fancy's wing:
  For far above her high career,
Upborne by worth the immortal chief shall rise,
  And to the lay-enraptur'd ear
Of Seraphs listening from th' empyreal sphere,
Glory, her hymn divine, shall carol through the skies.

For though the Muse in all unequal strain
  Sung of the wreaths that Albion's warriors bore
  From ev'ry region and from ev'y shore,
The naval triumphs of her George's reign—
  Triumphs by many a valiant son
  From Gaul, Iberia, and Batavia won;
  Or by St Vincent's rocky mound,
  Or sluggish Texel's shoaly sound;
  Or Haffnia's hyperborean wave,
  Or where Canopus' billows lave
  Th' Egyptian coast, while Albion's genius guides
  Her dauntless hero through the fav'ring tides,
  Where rocks, nor sands, nor tempests' roar,
  Nor batteries thundering from the shore,
  Arrest the fury of his naval war,
  When Glory shines the leading star;
Still higher deeds the lay recording claim,
Still rise Britannia's sons to more exalted fame.

The fervid source of heat and light
  Descending through the western skies,
Though veil'd awhile from mortal sight,
  Emerging soon with golden beams shall rise,
In orient climes with brighter radiance shine,
And sow th' ethereal plains with flame divine.
  So damp'd by Peace's transient smile,
  If Britain's glory seem to fade awhile,
  Yet when occasion's kindling rays
  Relumine valour's gen'rous blaze,
  Higher the radiant flames aspire,
And shine with clearer light and glow with fiercer fire.

From Europe's shores th' insidious train,
  Eluding Britain's watchful eye,
  Rapid across th' Atlantic fly
  To isles that stud the western main;
There proud their conqu'ring banners seem to rise,
And fann'd by shadowy triumphs flout the skies:
  But, lo! th' avenging Pow'r appears,
  His victor-flag immortal Nelson rears;
  Swift as the raven's ominous race
  Fly the strong eagle o'er th' ethereal space,
  The Gallic barks the billowy deep divide,
Their conquests lost in air, o'erwhelm'd in shame their pride.

The hour of vengeance comes—by Gades' tow'rs,
  By high Trafalgar's ever-trophied shore,
The godlike warrior on the adverse Pow'rs
  Leads his resistless fleet with daring prore,
Terrific as th' electric bolt that flies
With fatal shock athwart the thund'ring skies,
By the mysterious will of Heaven
On man's presuming offspring driven,
Full on the scatter'd foe he hurls his fires,
Performs the dread behest, and in the flash expires—

But not his fame—While chiefs who bleed
For sacred duty's holy meed,
With glory's amaranthine wreath,
By weeping Victory crown'd in death,
In History's awful page shall stand
Foremost amid th' heroic band;
NELSON! so long thy hallow'd name
Thy Country's gratitude shall claim;
And while a people's paeans raise
To thee the choral hymn of praise,
And while a patriot Monarch's tear
Bedews and sanctifies thy bier,
Each youth of martial hope shall feel
True valour's animating zeal;
With emulative wish thy trophies see,
And heroes, yet unborn, shall Britain owe to thee.

[10]

Robert Southey

(1774–1843)

For many people Robert Southey is the earliest of the laureates that they can recognize as a real person. Of course, they might feel closer to such a shadowy figure as Eusden or Pye if their lives were better documented. But the suspicion remains that nothing can penetrate the suffocating obscurity of their literary worlds. Southey, on the other hand, is real enough; at least the story of his development from revolutionary firebrand to diehard reactionary still arouses indignation or sympathy, according to point of view.

Southey (the name rhymes with mouthy) was born on 12 August 1774 in Bristol, where his father was a linen draper. He spent much of his childhood with a maiden aunt, Elizabeth Tyler, managing to read most of Shakespeare before he was eight. In 1788 his uncle, the Rev. Herbert Hill, who wanted him to become a clergyman, offered to pay for his education, and the boy was sent to Westminster School in London. He became an ardent supporter of the French Revolution, which began in 1789; but after four years he was expelled—for writing an essay against flogging.

In 1793, a year after his father died in debt, Southey went up to Balliol College, Oxford, where he was soon labelled a 'Jacobin', the equivalent today of being a 'communist'. Although he disliked the university, he was able to write quantities of verse, including a draft of his earliest epic, *Joan of Arc*. He soon decided that he could never become a Church of England minister.

When Samuel Taylor Coleridge, a couple of years his senior, chanced to visit Oxford in 1794, he and Southey became firm friends. Thus was born Pantisocracy, a plan to set up a mixed commune in the United States. The scheme never got beyond the discussion stage, however. Miss Tyler refused to have anything more to do with her nephew; she opposed both his involvement with the commune and his engagement to Edith Fricker, a Bristol girl, whose sister Mary had already married one of Southey's friends. Desperate for money, the two poets turned to journalism and to lecturing. But their plans soon disintegrated, and the friendship cooled, though not before a somewhat reluctant Coleridge had married Sara, the third Fricker sister, in October 1794. In November Southey married Edith, leaving immediately for Portugal, where his uncle, Mr Hill, was chaplain to the English community in Oporto.

Southey returned home the following May to find that *Joan of Arc*, published just before he left England, had made him well known. His political views were now changing, especially as the revolution in France continued to devour more and more of its children. He worked hard at a volume of letters describing his travels in Portugal, published more poetry, and eventually became reconciled with Coleridge. Early in 1797 he went to London to study law, but soon abandoned this for full-time writing and journalism. In 1800 he was back in Portugal, collecting material for a massive history. He returned to England the following year, even more opposed to Napoleon, and published a long epic poem with an Arabian theme, called *Thalaba, the Destroyer*.

In 1802 the Southeys' first child, a daughter, was born; but she lived only a year, dying shortly before they moved to Cumberland to join Coleridge, his wife Sara, and their three children at Greta Hall, Keswick. Wordsworth and his sister Dorothy were already installed 15 miles away at Grasmere. Soon after the move, Southey, now approaching 30, seems to have decided to concentrate on writing prose rather than verse. The choice could not have been easy; but he never forgot the struggles of his young days, and he was determined to support his family.

In 1809 Coleridge left his wife and family, and from then on the whole Greta Hall *ménage*, which included Mary, the other Fricker sister, became Southey's responsibility. Redoubling his efforts to support all these dependants, he became a regular contributor to the newly launched *Quarterly Review*, a Tory periodical that was to provide his basic income for almost 30 years. The radical fires of youth were now quite extinguished. But Southey was never a stereotype of the Tory diehard. As he wrote at the time: 'I wish for reform, because I cannot but see that all things are tending towards revolution, and nothing but reform can by any possibility prevent it.' By now many of his countrymen regarded him as one of the greatest of living poets.

In 1813, when Henry James Pye died, the Prince Regent, whose father George III was permanently insane, wanted to make Southey laureate. But owing to a bureaucratic blunder the post was first offered—by the prime minister, Lord Liverpool—to Walter Scott. Scott declined, but suggested that Southey, a friend of his for several years, was the best candidate. So, in the end, the Regent had his way. The laureateship now carried a salary of only £100, but Southey invested the money in an insurance policy for his family. (He was already paying £56 in tax on a government pension he had been given in 1807.) The new laureate tried hard to end the obligatory poems—'I would not write odes as boys write exercises, at stated times and upon stated subjects . . .'—but nothing was done until 1820, when the death of George III brought the custom to an end.

The year 1813 saw the publication of his *Life of Nelson* (still in print today) and was also the occasion of his first meeting with Lord Byron, who wrote in his journal: 'His prose is perfect. Of his poetry there are various opinions: there is, perhaps, too much of it for the present generation; posterity will probably select. He has *passages* equal to anything.'

In April 1816 the death of his only son, aged nine, came as a cruel blow from which Southey never entirely recovered. Later that same year he learnt that the prime minister was willing to offer him a well-paid journalistic post. But he had no wish to become a party hack and turned down the offer. The following spring John Walter, proprietor of *The Times* (founded 1785), tried—indirectly—to persuade him to accept the editorship. This approach, too, was rejected, even though Southey had no idea that Walter (as we now know) was prepared to offer a salary of around £2,000.

Eight years later the publication of Southey's *A Vision of Judgement* (1821), written in commemoration of George III, set off one of the most famous explosions in the history of literary warfare.

Southey's description of the king's arrival at the gates of heaven is certainly fatuous; but he also provided a preface attacking the Satanic school of poets, his epithet for Byron, Shelley, and their followers. Byron of course regarded Southey as the embodiment of Tory stupidity and stubbornness, and—quite inaccurately—as the author of an attack on Shelley in the *Quarterly Review*.

In his rejoinder, entitled *The Vision of Judgment*, Byron treated the laureate without mercy. Not only did he ridicule Southey's vanity and (in this case) his metrical incompetence; he went farther and charged him with that unforgiveable literary sin—boredom. The dénoument comes when Southey begins to read his own *Vision* to the heavenly host and assembled devils. Everyone flees in horror, and in the confusion the aged monarch slips unnoticed through the gates.

The laureate's financial worries virtually ended in 1835, when the prime minister, Sir Robert Peel, increased his government pension by £300 a year. But Southey's wife had become insane in 1834 and her death three years later shattered him. Among his last works was a rambling miscellany called *The Doctor*, which eventually ran to seven volumes. It contains the story of *The Three Bears*, which modern research has finally shown not to be an original work of Southey's, though he can claim every credit for making it one of the most famous of all nursery tales.

In 1839 he married Caroline Bowles, a poet he had corresponded with for more than 20 years. Their happiness was short-lived. Within a matter of weeks it was clear that Southey's mind was giving way, and by the next summer he had become virtually senile. He died on 21 March 1843 and was buried at Crosthwaite, outside Keswick. Wordsworth, who came to the funeral, later supplied 18 lines of verse for the monument in the church.

Funeral Song for the Princess Charlotte of Wales 1817

'What an extinction of youth and happiness!' wrote the diarist Fanny Burney on learning of the death in childbirth of the 21-year-old Princess Charlotte on 6 November 1817, at Claremont in Surrey. The princess was the only child of the Prince Regent (later George IV) and therefore heiress presumptive to the throne. Her death caused an immense outburst of national grief. The Regent had deserted her mother, Princess Caroline of Brunswick, soon after their marriage, and his subsequent treatment of his wife had added to his already immense unpopularity. Princess Charlotte had married Prince Leopold of Saxe-Coburg, on 2 May 1816. He was the brother of the German-born duchess of Kent, who later became Queen Victoria's mother. In 1831 he became the first king of the newly independent Belgium.

In its summer pride array'd,
Low our Tree of Hope is laid!
Low it lies:—in evil hour,
Visiting the bridal bower,
Death hath levell'd root and flower.
Windsor, in thy sacred shade,
(This the end of pomp and power!)
Have the rites of death been paid;
Windsor, in thy sacred shade
Is the Flower of Brunswick laid!

Ye whose relics rest around,
Tenants of this funeral ground!
Know ye, Spirits, who is come,
By immitigable doom
Summon'd to the untimely tomb?
Late with youth and splendour crown'd,
Late in beauty's vernal bloom,
Late with love and joyaunce blest;
Never more lamented guest
Was in Windsor laid to rest.

Henry, thou of saintly worth,
Thou, to whom thy Windsor gave
Nativity, and name, and grave;
Thou art in this hallowed earth
Cradled for the immortal birth!
Heavily upon his head
Ancestral crimes were visited:
He, in spirit like a child,
Meek of heart and undefiled,
Patiently his crown resign'd,
And fix'd on heaven his heavenly mind,
Blessing, while he kiss'd the rod,
His Redeemer and his God.
Now many he in realms of bliss
Greet a soul as pure as his.

Passive as that humble spirit,
Lies his bold dethroner too;
A dreadful debt did he inherit
To his injured lineage due;
Ill-starr'd prince, whose martial merit
His own England long might rue!
Mournful was that Edward's fame,
Won in fields contested well,
While he sought his rightful claim:
Witness Aire's unhappy water,
Where the ruthless Clifford fell;
And when Wharfe ran red with slaughter
On the day of Towton's field,
Gathering, in its guilty flood,
The carnage and the ill-spilt blood
That forty thousand lives could yield.
Cressy was to this but sport,—
Poictiers but a pageant vain;
And the victory of Spain
Seem'd a strife for pastime meant,
And the work of Agincourt

Only like a tournament;
Half the blood which there was spent
Had sufficed again to gain
Anjou and ill-yielded Maine,
Normandy and Aquitaine;
And Our Lady's ancient towers,
Maugre all the Valois' powers,
Had a second time been ours.—
A gentle daughter of thy line,
Edward, lays her dust with thine.

Thou, Elizabeth, art here;
Thou to whom all griefs were known;
Who wert placed upon the bier
In happier hour than on the throne.
Fatal daughter, fatal mother,
Raised to that ill-omen'd station,
Father, uncle, sons, and brother,
Mourn'd in blood her elevation!
Woodville, in the realms of bliss,
To thine offspring thou may'st say,
Early death is happiness;
And favour'd in their lot are they
Who are not left to learn below
That length of life is length of woe.
Lightly let this ground be prest;
A broken heart is here at rest.

But thou, Seymour, with a greeting,
Such as sisters use at meeting,
Joy, and sympathy, and love,
Wilt hail her in the seats above.
Like in loveliness were ye,
By a like lamented doom,
Hurried to an early tomb.

While together, spirits blest,
Here your earthly relics rest,
Fellow angels shall ye be
In the angelic company.

Henry, too, hath here his part;
At the gentle Seymour's side,
With his best beloved bride
Cold and quiet, here are laid
The ashes of that fiery heart.
Not with his tyrannic spirit
Shall our Charlotte's soul inherit;
No, by Fisher's hoary head,—
By More, the learned and the good,—
By Katharine's wrongs and Boleyn's blood,—
By the life so basely shed
Of the pride of Norfolk's line,
By the axe so often red,
By the fire with martyrs fed.
Hateful Henry, not with thee
May her happy spirit be!

And here lies one whose tragic name
A reverential thought may claim;
That murder'd Monarch, whom the grave,
Revealing its long secret, gave
Again to sight, that we might spy
His comely face, and waking eye!
There, thrice fifty years, it lay,
Exempt from natural decay,
Unclosed and bright, as if to say,
A plague of bloodier, baser birth,
Than that beneath whose rage he bled
Was loose upon our guilty earth;—
Such awful warning from the dead,
Was given by that portentous eye;
Then it closed eternally.

Ye whose relics rest around,
Tenants of this funeral ground;
Even in your immortal spheres,
What fresh yearnings will ye feel,
When this earthly guest appears!
Us she leaves in grief and tears;
But to you will she reveal
Tidings of old England's weal;
Of a righteous war pursued,
Long, through evil and through good,
With unshaken fortitude;
Of peace in battle twice achieved;
Of her fiercest foe subdued,
And Europe from the yoke reliev'd,
Upon that Brabantine plain!
Such the proud, the virtuous story,
Such the great, the endless glory,
Of her father's splendid reign!
He who wore the sable mail,
Might at this heroic tale,
Wish himself on earth again.

One who reverently, for thee,
Raised the strain of bridal verse,
Flower of Brunswick! mournfully
Lays a garland on thy herse.

On the Death of Queen Charlotte 1818

Queen Charlotte, born in 1744, had been married to George III since 1761 and died at Kew on 17 November 1818, just over a year before the old, blind, insane king himself. Their married life had been happy, stable, and above reproach—in striking contrast to the conduct of their sons.

DEATH has gone up into our Palaces!
The light of day once more
Hath visited the last abode
Of mortal royalty,
The dark and silent vault.

But not as when the silence of that vault
Was interrupted last
Doth England raise her loud lament,
Like one by sudden grief
Surprised and overcome.

Then with a passionate sorrow we bewail'd
Youth on the untimely bier;
And hopes which seem'd like flower-buds full,
Just opening to the sun,
For ever swept away.

The heart then struggled with repining thoughts,
With feelings that almost
Arraign'd the inscrutable decree,
Embittered by a sense
Of that which might have been.

This grief hath no repining; all is well,
What hath been, and what is.
The Angel of Deliverance came
To one who full of years
Awaited her release.

All that our fathers in their prayers desired,
When first their chosen Queen
Set on our shores her happy feet,
All by indulgent Heaven
Had largely been vouchsafed.

At Court the Household Virtues had their place;
Domestic Purity
Maintain'd her proper influence there:
The marriage bed was blest,
And length of days was given.

No cause for sorrow then, but thankfulness;
Life's business well perform'd,
When weary age full willingly
Resigns itself to sleep,
In sure and certain hope!

Oh end to be desired, whene'er, as now,
Good works have gone before,
The seasonable fruit of Faith;
And good Report, and good
Example have survived.

Her left hand knew not of the ample alms
Which her right hand had done;
And therefore in the aweful hour,
The promises were hers
To secret bounty made.

With more than royal honours to the tomb
Her bier is borne; with more
Than Pomp can claim, or Power bestow;
With blessings and with prayers
From many a grateful heart.

Long, long then shall Queen Charlotte's name be dear;
And future Queens to her
As to their best examplar look;
Who imitates her best
May best deserve our love.

[11]

William Wordsworth

(1770–1850)

When William Wordsworth succeeded Robert Southey as laureate, he became—at 73—the oldest poet ever to accept the post. But although he held office for seven years—an appointment now without official duties—he did not contribute a single poem. His collected works, it is true, include an ode written in 1847; but, as we shall see, that piece was not his own.

Wordsworth's long life (1770–1850) coincided with an explosive moment in Western history. The Industrial Revolution was well under way before he was born. When he was six, the American Revolution established the first modern democracy; and when he was 19, the French Revolution toppled the most absolute monarchy in Europe. By the time he was an old man the whole basis of industrial production had altered—workers lived in towns rather than in villages, and spent their lives in factories; six million acres of common land had been enclosed.

Change was not confined just to the structure of society. The long reign of classicism, with its rigid values and literary forms, was also drawing to an end. In its place appeared the Romantic movement, hymning the individual and stressing the supremacy of imagination rather than reason.

William Wordsworth was born at Cockermouth in Cumberland on 7 April 1770. His father, John Wordsworth, was agent to Sir James Lowther, first earl of Lonsdale, an immensely rich landowner. In March 1778 William's mother died. William, his elder brother Richard, and his two younger brothers, John and Christopher, were sent in turn as boarders to the grammar school at Hawkshead in Lancashire. They lived there in lodgings, but spent the holidays either with the Cooksons, their mother's parents, whom William detested, or with an uncle. To make matters worse, their sister Dorothy, 20 months younger than William, was sent to live with cousins in Halifax, Yorkshire.

In 1783 the children's father died, leaving almost nothing. Most of his savings—some £5,000—had gone in loans to his half-mad employer, who refused to pay anything back. (The money was not returned until 1802, when the first earl died.) The children now became wards of two uncles, and were miserable. William seems to have suffered most, and made long excursions into the nearby Lake district, finding some relief for his loss in the wild beauty of the lakes and mountains. Once acquired, this wandering habit remained with him all his life.

Wordsworth's earliest surviving poems date from Hawkshead, where a sympathetic headmaster introduced him to poetry. In 1787 the Wordsworth boys were at last reunited with their sister, and William went up to St John's College, Cambridge.

When the French Revolution began in 1789, there were many English people who welcomed it; they thought it would lead to greater political freedom throughout Europe. William himself visited France in 1790, finding the whole nation 'mad with joy in consequence of the revolution'. In November 1791 he returned to France, remaining in Orléans and Blois, south of Paris, most of the following year. There he met Michel Armand Beaupuy, an officer who converted him to the revolutionary cause. And he fell in love with Annette Vallon, daughter of a barber-surgeon. At 25, she was four years older than William, and she soon became pregnant. Although the lovers planned to marry, William went back to England just before their daughter Caroline was born. No doubt, he had intended to collect Annette and her daughter, but within weeks England and France were at war. In 1802, when peace returned, William, accompanied by Dorothy, met Annette in Calais. But feelings had cooled, and the lovers parted. When Caroline eventually married, however, her father contributed to her dowry.

This affair with Annette remained a secret for more than a century; but the whole experience—to say nothing of the need to conceal it and to come to terms with his feelings of guilt—scarred Wordsworth for life. Gradually, too, he came to accept the fact of war with France, for he found it impossible to condone the Reign of Terror or the emergence of Napoleon as dictator.

In 1795, with the help of a legacy, William and Dorothy settled in Dorset, later moving to Somerset to be closer to Coleridge, who became a potent influence on Wordsworth's rapidly developing poetic genius. Together the two men produced *Lyrical Ballads* (1798), the embodiment of a new poetic faith. The introduction to this anonymous work explained that most of the poems were experiments, 'written chiefly with a view to ascertain how far the language of conversation in the middle and lower classes of society is adapted to the purpose of poetic pleasures'. Coleridge dealt with the supernatural or romantic themes (*The Ancient Mariner* and two other poems), while Wordsworth supplied poems designed 'to give the charm of novelty to things of every day'. The first edition had little impact (only 500 copies were printed), even though it marked a significant stage in the development of the Romantic movement in England. But when a second edition appeared in 1800, Wordsworth, whose name appeared on the title page, supplied the preface; it contains his famous statement that poetry is 'the spontaneous overflow of powerful feelings: it takes its origin from emotion recollected in tranquillity'.

In 1799, after visiting Germany, Wordsworth and Dorothy settled at Dove Cottage, Grasmere, in the Lake district. The following summer Coleridge and his wife Sara came to live at Keswick, 15 miles away, where they were later joined by the Southeys.

William and Dorothy, 'his exquisite sister', as Coleridge called her, were by now passionately attached to one another. They had always been affectionate, but the break with Annette drew them even closer. Dorothy, who was convinced of her brother's genius, wanted only to dedicate her life to his advancement. In short, brother and sister fell in love, and the only way William could escape the unthinkable implications of such a relationship was to relegate the whole affair to his subconscious. His own inner life became the sole focus of his thoughts, and this led him to write a number of magnificent poems, all associated in some way with his experiences as a child. He finally won through; but for his sister the outlook was bleak. However, when William married Mary

Hutchinson, a childhood friend, in 1802, and began to raise a family, Dorothy became part of a *ménage à trois* that was apparently without jealousy. But in 1829, her health broke down; by 1835 she was unable to walk and her mind became affected. She died in 1855, a victim of arteriosclerosis.

For William the years from 1797 to 1805 were a period of intense creation; but thereafter inspiration began to desert him. Perhaps it was the price he paid in order to come to terms with life, the only way he could resolve his emotional crises.

In 1807 *Poems in Two Volumes* were published. Although they included such fine sonnets as *On Westminster Bridge* and *To Milton*, as well as *Resolution and Independence*, and the odes *To Duty* and *Intimations of Immortality*, the book came in for a lot of ridicule. So much so, that Wordsworth published nothing for the next eight years. His long autobiographical poem, *The Prelude*, begun in 1799, was complete by 1805; but it remained unpublished until after his death. *The Excursion*, part of a projected philosophical poem 'on man, on nature and on human life', was published in 1814.

The years of poetic decline were comparatively uneventful. In 1813 Wordsworth became Distributor of Stamps for Westmorland, an inland revenue post worth about £400 a year, so the family were able to move to Rydal Mount, two miles away, where he lived for the rest of his life.

In 1843, when Wordsworth was asked to become poet laureate, he at first refused. Southey, he remembered, had supplied public poems on different occasions and had been worried by his failure to write something for Victoria's coronation. But Sir Robert Peel, the prime minister, allayed his fears by promising 'you shall have nothing *required* of you'.

In 1847, however, when the Prince Consort was to be inaugurated Chancellor of Cambridge University, Wordsworth was asked to write a poem. Although he disapproved of Albert's advanced views on education, a poem was indeed supplied; but the author was Edward Quillinan, who had married the poet's favourite daughter Dora in 1841. Dora, now 43, lay dying, and her distraught father handed the assignment to his son-in-law. He himself confined his efforts to corrections and revisions.

The fact that Wordsworth wrote nothing during his period of office cannot diminish the long-term value of his contribution to the laureateship. The enormous prestige associated with his name did far more to raise the status of the post than any number of public poems he might have written in the last years of his life, which finally ended at Grasmere—where he lies buried—on 23 April 1850.

The Installation of Prince Albert as Chancellor of Cambridge University 1847

This ode, the only official poem written during Wordsworth's tenure of office, was in fact composed by his son-in-law, Edward Quillinan. At the time, Wordsworth's daughter, Dora, was striken by a fatal illness, and her father was unable to tackle the commission himself. The ode begins with a brief reference to the ending of the war against Napoleon in 1815, and then goes on to review the unusual set of circumstances by which Victoria came to the throne in 1837 at the age of 18.

She would not have become queen had not Princess Charlotte died in childbirth in 1818, the year before Victoria was born. Charlotte was heiress presumptive to the Prince Regent (later George IV) and wife of Prince Leopold of Saxe-Coburg, brother of Victoria's mother. (See *Southey's poem, p. 117). The deaths of Victoria's father, the duke of Kent, in 1820, and of her cousins, two daughters of the duke of Clarence, in 1819 and 1821, made it almost certain that she would eventually succeed. In 1830, when the duke of Clarence was crowned William IV, she became heiress presumptive.*

Prince Albert, second son of the duke of Saxe-Coburg-Gotha, was the same age as Victoria and her first cousin. Their uncle Prince Leopold, who became king of Belgium in 1831, had always hoped the two would marry, which they did in February 1840.

The reference to Luther towards the end of the ode was a timely reminder that Albert's ancestors had been almost alone in upholding the Protestant cause from its outset.

Introduction and chorus

For thirst of power that Heaven disowns,
For temples, towers, and thrones,
Too long insulted by the Spoiler's shock,
Indignant Europe cast
Her stormy foe at last
To reap the whirlwind on a Libyan rock.

Solo—(tenor)

War is passion's basest game
Madly played to win a name;
Up starts some tyrant, Earth and Heaven to dare.
The servile million bow;
But will the lightning glance aside to spare
The Despot's laurelled brow?

Chorus

War is mercy, glory, fame,
Waged in Freedom's holy cause;
Freedom, such as Man may claim
Under God's restraining laws.
Such is Albion's fame and glory:
Let rescued Europe tell the story.

Recitativo (accompanied)—(contralto)

But lo, what sudden cloud has darkened all
The land as with a funeral pall?
The Rose of England suffers blight,
The flower has drooped, the Isle's delight,
Flower and bud together fall—
A Nation's hopes lie crushed in Claremont's desolate hall.

Air—(soprano)

Time a chequered mantle wears;—
Earth awakes from wintry sleep;
Again the Tree a blossom bears—
Cease, Britannia, cease to weep!

Hark to the peals on this bright May morn!
They tell that your future Queen is born.

Soprano solo and chorus

A Guardian Angel fluttered
Above the Babe, unseen;
One word he softly uttered—
It named the future Queen:
And a joyful cry through the Island rang,
As clear and bold as the trumpet's clang,
As bland as the reed of peace—
'VICTORIA be her name!'
For righteous triumphs are the base
Whereon Britannia rests her peaceful fame.

Quartet

Time, in his mantle's sunniest fold,
Uplifted in his arms the child;
And, while the fearless Infant smiled,
Her happier destiny foretold:—
'Infancy, by Wisdom mild,
Trained to health and artless beauty;
Youth, by pleasure unbeguiled
From the lore of lofty duty;
Womanhood is pure renown,
Seated on her lineal throne:
Leaves of myrtle in her Crown,
Fresh with lustre all their own,
Love, the treasure worth possessing,
More than all the world beside,
This shall be her choicest blessing,
Oft to royal hearts denied.'

Recitativo (accompanied)—(bass)

That eve, the Star of Brunswick shone
With stedfast ray benign
On Gotha's ducal roof, and on
The softly flowing Leine;

Nor failed to gild the spires of Bonn,
  And glittered on the Rhine—
Old Camus, too, on that prophetic night
  Was conscious of the ray;
And his willows whispered in its light,
  Not to the Zephyr's sway,
But with a Delphic life, in sight
  Of this auspicious day:

Chorus

This day, when Granta hails her chosen Lord,
  And proud of her award,
  Confiding in the Star serene,
Welcomes the Consort of a happy Queen.

Air—(contralto)

Prince, in these Collegiate bowers,
Where Science, leagued with holier truth,
Guards the sacred heart of youth,
Solemn monitors are ours.
These reverend aisles, these hallowed towers,
Raised by many a hand august,
Are haunted by majestic Powers,
The memories of the Wise and Just,
Who, faithful to a pious trust,
Here, in the Founder's spirit sought
To mould and stamp the ore of thought
In that bold form and impress high
That best betoken patriot loyalty.
Not in vain those Sages taught,—
True disciples, good as great,
Have pondered here their country's weal,
Weighed the Future by the Past,
Learned how social frames may last,
And how a Land may rule its fate
By constancy inviolate,

Though worlds to their foundations reel
The sport of factious Hate or godless Zeal.

Air—(bass)

Albert, in thy race we cherish
A Nation's strength that will not perish
While England's sceptred Line
True to the King of Kings is found;
Like that Wise ancestor of thine
Who threw the Saxon shield o'er Luther's life,
When first above the yells of bigot strife
The trumpet of the Living Word
Assumed a voice of deep portentous sound,
From gladdened Elbe to startled Tiber heard.

Chorus

What shield more sublime
E'er was blazoned or sung?
And the PRINCE whom we greet
From its Hero is sprung.
Resound, resound the strain,
That hails him for our own!
Again, again, and yet again,
For the Church, the State, the Throne!
And that Presence fair and bright,
Ever blest wherever seen,
Who deigns to grace our festal rite,
The pride of the Islands, VICTORIA THE QUEEN.

[12]

Alfred, Lord Tennyson

(1809–1892)

With Alfred Tennyson we come to the most distinguished of all the laureates. Not only did he hold office longer—for 42 years—than anyone else, he was also the first British poet to become a truly national figure in his own lifetime. To the laureateship he brought a moral obligation and an enthusiasm that have never been equalled, and these qualities, coupled with his deep sense of mission, made him more than eager to write verses on a wide range of national issues and occasions.

Born on 6 August 1809, Tennyson was the fourth of 12 children. He grew up in the Lincolnshire village of Somersby, where his father, a man embittered by having been disinherited by his father, was rector. At the age of seven he was sent to nearby Louth to join his brothers Frederick and Charles at school. But after four unhappy years he returned home, remaining there until he went up to Trinity College, Cambridge, in February 1828.

To begin with, Tennyson was too shy to take part in college life, but at the end of his first year, he joined the Apostles, a debating club consisting of 12 members, many of them destined to become famous in Victorian society. Tennyson, six-foot tall, with dark hair, and much addicted to pipe smoking, soon made his mark, and his poetry was much admired.

In October 1828 Arthur Hallam, a gifted and handsome youth of 17, joined Trinity College. He became Tennyson's dearest companion, and an intense, emotional relationship gradually developed between them, which was to affect the poet for the rest of his life. In June 1829 Tennyson, who was studying history, classics, and natural science, won the Chancellor's medal for a poem on Timbuctoo. Giving the news to his friend William Gladstone (the future prime minister) then at Oxford, Hallam wrote: 'I consider

Tennyson as promising fair to be the greatest poet of our generation, perhaps of our century.' Convincing evidence for Hallam's claim appeared in June 1830 with the publication of *Poems, chiefly Lyrical*, an astonishing achievement for a young man of 21.

In March 1831 Tennyson's father died, and Alfred left Cambridge without taking a degree. Luckily, the family were allowed to remain in the rectory another six years. In the summer of 1832 he visited Germany with Hallam, returning for the publication of his new book, *Poems*. This included *The Lotus Eaters* and *The Lady of Shallot*; but reviewers were not impressed. Indeed so hostile were the notices, Tennyson refused to publish anything new for almost ten years.

But this was as nothing compared to the shattering news of Hallam's death—in September 1833, at the age of 22. In time Tennyson came to terms with his loss, finding release in intense spells of creativity. His family too shared his grief, for Hallam had been engaged to Tennyson's sister Emily for over a year.

All was not despair, however. In May 1836 Tennyson fell in love with Emily Sellwood as he escorted her at the wedding of her sister Louisa to his brother Charles. Unfortunately, Emily's parents were not eager for her to marry a poet; and despite an engagement in 1838, the lovers were forced to part in 1840. Ten years elapsed before they were free to marry, when Emily was 37 and Tennyson 40. This painful separation, allied to his grief over Hallam, affected Tennyson profoundly; but his strong religious faith and his determination not to go under bore him up. In 1842 the publication of *Poems* (in two volumes) established him as a major poetic force. But recognition, however welcome, brought no material compensation. Indeed, Tennyson became almost penniless after investing most of his small capital in a 'Patent Decorative Carving Company', which collapsed after a few months. He became profoundly depressed and his health started to suffer. Above all, he feared he might succumb to epilepsy and alcoholism, afflictions that were hereditary in the Tennyson family. But things improved in 1845, when Sir Robert Peel, the prime minister, was persuaded to grant him a pension of £200.

His next publication was *The Princess* (1847), a long poem about the emancipation of women. But the poet could not bring himself to champion such a cause; his views on the subject were echoed by most Victorian husbands:

> Man for the sword and for the needle she:
> Man with the head and woman with the heart;
> Man to command and woman to obey;
> All else confusion.

Interest in the poem today is confined largely to the 1850 edition, for to this Tennyson added six enchanting lyrics, including *Sweet and low*, *The splendour falls on castle walls*, and *Now sleeps the crimson petal, now the white*.

The year 1850 was in fact something of an *annus mirabilis* for Tennyson. On 1 June *In Memoriam*, poems written over the years in memory of Hallam, was published; on 13 June he married Emily; and on 19 November Queen Victoria appointed him poet laureate. *In Memoriam* was published anonymously, but its author was easily identified, and the poem's many admirers included Prince Albert, the queen's husband. Like so much of Tennyson's work, this poem bears witness to his familiarity with science and its increasing impact on society. Above all, the poem raised, in memorable language, all the issues associated with the idea of a personal God and survival after death. But the poem was not without its critics. Tennyson's old Cambridge friend Edward FitzGerald, translator of *The Rubaiyat of Omar Khayyám* (1859), said it was full of the finest things; but he thought it had the air of being evolved by a poetical machine of the highest order.

Wordsworth's death in April 1850 created all the usual problems involved in finding a new laureate. The position was offered first to Samuel Rogers, more renowned for his literary breakfasts than for his poetry. But at 87 Rogers was too old and recommended Tennyson. After a day's hesitation, the poet accepted. On 6 March 1851, attired in the court dress worn by his predecessor—like Wordsworth, he borrowed it from Rogers—he went to Buckingham Palace for an audience with the queen. His dedication, his patriotism, and his interest in science (he was elected a Fellow of the Royal Society in 1865) made him an ideal choice. But despite these qualifications Tennyson found that his first official utterance, the *Ode on the Death of the Duke of Wellington*, published as a two-shilling pamphlet on 18 November 1850, the day of the funeral, met with little approval.

In 1853 the Tennysons, with their one-year-old son, Hallam, moved into Farringford, a house at Freshwater, Isle of Wight. Here the laureate spent the greater part of his many remaining years, producing an astonishing amount of work. The outbreak of the Crimean war in 1854 (the year his second son Lionel was born) stimulated his interest in imperial and patriotic issues. Most memorably, *The Times* report of 2 December 1854, describing the charge of the light brigade at Balaclava, inspired the best known of all his poems. *Idylls of the King* (1859), further evidence of his continuing interest in Arthurian legend, brought him fame and popularity on a scale hitherto undreamt of by an English poet. Although these Arthurian poems embody many of his views on Victorian society, they also provided a convenient escape from the realities of a society divided, in the words of the *Communist Manifesto* (1848), 'into two great classes directly facing each other—bourgeoisie and proletariat'. In December 1861, when the Prince Consort, one of the poem's greatest admirers, died, Tennyson wrote a special dedication to him, which was published soon after, with the second edition. This led to his first interview, as laureate, with Victoria, and laid the foundations of a long and deepening friendship.

By 1864 Tennyson had become a cult figure, his immense popularity further enhanced by *Enoch Arden, and other Poems*, which sold 60,000 copies within weeks and netted him £6,000 in its first year. Publicity seekers were now besieging Farringford, so in 1868 the Tennysons chose a site on the Surrey–Sussex border near Haslemere, and there built their second home, Aldworth.

During his remaining years, the laureate supplied numerous official poems, but this took only a fraction of his time. Energetic as ever, he now began to write verse plays for the London theatre; but nothing could match his non-dramatic work. In his 71st year he produced *Ballads and Poems*, which included *The Revenge*, his rousing account of a famous sea battle. In 1884 Gladstone, now premier, offered him a peerage. He accepted, so becoming the first English peer to owe his title to poetry. Two years later Lionel died on his way home from India, and was buried at sea. Tennyson managed to survive even this bereavement, and when over 80 he wrote *Crossing the Bar*, the most famous of all his short poems; his son Hallam, now his father's companion and secretary, called it the crown of his life's work. He died at Aldworth on 6 October 1892, his hand resting on his Shakespeare, the moon flooding the room with light. Laid to rest in Westminster Abbey, he was mourned by millions.

The Charge of the Light Brigade

This suicidal charge down a mile-long valley took place at Balaclava on 25 October 1854, during the Crimean war. In mid-November Tennyson had read an account of the action in The Times, *written by William Russell, the paper's influential war correspondent. Two weeks later, he wrote the poem, taking no more than a few minutes, and sent it to* The Examiner, *a weekly periodical, which printed it on 9 December. In 1855 some 2,000 copies of the poem were distributed to the British troops besieging Sebastopol. Of the 673 men who took part in the charge, 113 were killed and 134 wounded; 497 horses were destroyed. From beginning to end, the charge took 25 minutes.*

Half a league, half a league,
Half a league onward,
All in the valley of Death
  Rode the six hundred.
'Forward, the Light Brigade!
Charge for the guns!' he said:
Into the valley of Death
  Rode the six hundred.

'Forward, the Light Brigade!'
Was there a man dismay'd?
Not tho' the soldier knew
  Someone had blunder'd:
Their's not to make reply,
Their's not to reason why,
Their's but to do and die:
Into the valley of Death
  Rode the six hundred.

Cannon to right of them,
Cannon to left of them,
Cannon in front of them
  Volley'd and thunder'd;
Storm'd at with shot and shell,
Boldly they rode and well,
Into the jaws of Death,
Into the mouth of Hell
  Rode the six hundred.

Flash'd all their sabres bare,
Flash'd as they turn'd in air,
Sabring the gunners there,
Charging an army, while
  All the world wonder'd:
Plunged in the battery-smoke
Right thro' the line they broke;
Cossack and Russian
Reel'd from the sabre-stroke
  Shatter'd and sunder'd.
Then they rode back, but not,
  Not the six hundred.

Cannon to the right of them,
Cannon to the left of them,
Cannon behind them
  Volley'd and thunder'd;

Storm'd at with shot and shell,
While horse and hero fell,
They that had fought so well
Came thro' the jaws of Death
Back from the mouth of Hell,
All that was left of them,
  Left of the six hundred.

When can their glory fade?
O the wild charge they made!
  All the world wonder'd.
Honour the charge they made!
Honour the Light Brigade,
  Noble six hundred!

The Charge of the Heavy Brigade

Written at the suggestion of Alexander Kinglake, author of an eight-volume history (1863–87) of the Crimean war, this poem appeared in March 1882 in Macmillan's Magazine. *On 25 October, 1854, at Balaclava, led by General Sir James Scarlett, some 500 troopers charged several hundred yards uphill to attack the main body of Russian cavalry—3,000 to 4,000 strong. After eight minutes, the enemy broke and fled. The 'gallant three hundred' (Scots Greys and Inniskillings) formed the first line of the brigade; the 'three' were Lieut. Alexander Elliot (Scarlett's aide-de-camp), a trumpeter, and an orderly.*

The charge of the gallant three hundred, the Heavy Brigade!
Down the hill, down the hill, thousands of Russians,
Thousands of horsemen, drew to the valley—and stay'd;
For Scarlett and Scarlett's three hundred were riding by
When the points of the Russian lances arose in the sky;
And he call'd 'Left wheel into line!' and they wheel'd and obey'd.

Then he look'd at the host that had halted he knew not why,
And he turn'd half round, and he bad his trumpeter sound
To the charge, and he rode on ahead, as he waved his blade
To the gallant three hundred whose glory will never die—
'Follow', and up the hill, up the hill, up the hill,
Follow'd the Heavy Brigade.

The trumpet, the gallop, the charge, and the might of the fight!
Thousands of horsemen had gather'd there on the height,
With a wing push'd out to the left and a wing to the right,
And who shall escape if they close? but he dash'd up alone
Thro' the great gray slope of men,
Sway'd his sabre, and held his own
Like an Englishman there and then;
All in a moment follow'd with force
Three that were next in their fiery course,
Wedged themselves in between horse and horse,
Fought for their lives in the narrow gap they had made—
Four amid thousands! and up the hill, up the hill,
Gallopt the gallant three hundred, the Heavy Brigade.

Fell like a cannonshot,
Burst like a thunderbolt,
Crash'd like a hurricane,
Broke thro' the mass from below,
Drove thro' the midst of the foe,
Plunged up and down, to and fro,
Rode flashing blow upon blow,
Brave Inniskillens and Greys
Whirling their sabres in circles of light!
And some of us, all in amaze,
Who were held for a while from the fight,
And were only standing at gaze,
When the dark-muffled Russian crowd
Folded its wings from the left and the right,
And roll'd them around like a cloud—
O mad for the charge and the battle were we,

When our own good redcoats sank from sight,
Like drops of blood in a dark-gray sea,
And we turn'd to each other, whispering, all dismay'd,
'Lost are the gallant three hundred of Scarlett's Brigade!'

'Lost one and all' were the words
Mutter'd in our dismay;
But they rode like Victors and Lords
Thro' the forest of lances and swords
In the heart of the Russian hordes,
They rode, or they stood at bay—
Struck with the sword-hand and slew,
Down with the bridle-hand drew
The foe from the saddle and threw
Underfoot there in the fray—
Ranged like a storm or stood like a rock
In the wave of a stormy day;
Till suddenly shock upon shock
Stagger'd the mass from without,
Drove it in wild disarray,
For our men gallopt up with a cheer and a shout,
And the foeman surged, and waver'd, and reel'd
Up the hill, up the hill, up the hill, out of the field,
And over the brow and away.

Glory to each and to all, and the charge that they made!
Glory to all the three hundred, and all the Brigade!

A Welcome to Alexandra

This was written in honour of the wedding of the prince of Wales (later Edward VII) to the princess Alexandra, daughter of Christian IX, king of Denmark, which took place at Windsor on 10 March 1863, the day the poem appeared in The Times. *The bride was 18, the bridegroom 21. As with several of the marriages of Victoria's children, this was an arranged match. Tennyson himself had been invited to the ceremony, but missed it because his invitation ticket arrived too late. Victoria, who had refused to allow the wedding to take place in London, remained hidden from view in a gallery above the aisle. The honeymoon was spent at Osborne, Isle of Wight, and Parliament voted the prince £100,000 a year.*

Sea-Kings' daughter from over the sea,
Alexandra!
Saxon and Norman and Dane are we,
But all of us Danes in our welcome of thee,
Alexandra!
Welcome her, thunders of fort and of fleet!
Welcome her, thundering cheer of the street!
Welcome her, all things youthful and sweet,
Scatter the blossom under her feet!
Break, happy land, into earlier flowers!
Make music, O bird, in the new-budded bowers!
Blazon your mottoes of blessing and prayer!
Welcome her, welcome her, all that is ours!
Warble, O bugle, and trumpet, blare!
Flags, flutter out upon turrets and towers!
Flames, on the windy headland flare!
Utter your jubilee, steeple and spire!
Clash, ye bells, in the merry March air!
Flash, ye cities, in rivers of fire!
Rush to the roof, sudden rocket, and higher
Melt into stars for the land's desire!
Roll and rejoice, jubilant voice,
Roll as a ground-swell dash'd on the strand,
Roar as the sea when he welcomes the land,
And welcome her, welcome the land's desire,
The sea-kings' daughter as happy as fair,
Blissful bride of a blissful heir,
Bride of the heir of the kings of the sea—
O joy to the people and joy to the throne,
Come to us, love us and make us your own:

For Saxon or Dane or Norman we,
Teuton or Celt, or whatever we be,
We are each all Dane in our welcome of thee,
Alexandra!

Riflemen, Form!

These verses, first entitled The War, *appeared in* The Times *on 9 May 1859, six days after France (in alliance with Piedmont, then an Italian kingdom) had declared war on Austria. The conflict, however, which was confined to Italy, lasted only three months. Tennyson shared a widespread fear of French invasion, so he was delighted when, three days after the publication of his poem, the secretary of war directed the lords-lieutenant of the counties to set up volunteer corps. The poem was adapted from verses Tennyson had written seven years before, when there were fears of a French invasion following the* coup d'état *that made Louis Napoleon, nephew of Napoleon I, dictator of France.*

There is a sound of thunder afar,
Storm in the South that darkens the day!
Storm of battle and thunder of war!
Well if it do not roll our way.
Storm, Storm, Riflemen form!
Ready, be ready against the storm!
Riflemen, Riflemen, Riflemen form!

Be not deaf to the sound that warns,
Be not gull'd by a despot's plea!
Are figs of thistles? or grapes of thorns?
How can a despot feel with the Free?

Form, Form, Riflemen Form
Ready, be ready to meet the storm!
Riflemen, Riflemen, Riflemen form!

Let your reforms for a moment go!
Look to your butts, and take good aims!
Better a rotten borough or so
Than a rotten fleet and a city in flames!
Storm, Storm, Riflemen form!
Ready, be ready against the storm!
Riflemen, Riflemen, Riflemen form!

Form, be ready to do or die!
Form in Freedom's name and the Queen's!
True we have got—*such* a faithful ally
That only the Devil can tell what he means.
Form, Form, Riflemen Form!
Ready, be ready to meet the storm!
Riflemen, Riflemen, Riflemen form!

The Fleet

Printed in The Times *on St George's Day 1885, and subtitled 'On its reported insufficiency', this was an attack on Lord Northbrook, the First Lord of the Admiralty. The subject could not have been more topical. In September 1884 the* Pall Mall Gazette *had started publishing articles about the declining strength of the Navy, and Gladstone's Liberal government was now under heavy fire from the Press. Indeed, after the publication, in 1871, of* The Battle of Dorking *(about an imaginary German attack on England), a spate of books appeared prophesying invasion. Since receiving his peerage in March 1884, Tennyson himself had become much involved in politics, and his opposition to Gladstone, an old friend, had intensified with the death of General Gordon at Khartoum in January 1885.*

You, you, *if* you shall fail to understand
  What England is, and what her all-in-all,
On you will come the curse of all the land,
  Should this old England fall
    Which Nelson left so great.

His isle, the mightiest Ocean-power on earth,
  Our own fair isle, the lord of every sea—
Her fuller franchise—what would that be worth—
  Her ancient fame of Free—
    Were she . . . a fallen state?

Her dauntless army scatter'd, and so small,
  Her island-myriads fed from alien lands—
The fleet of England is her all-in-all;
  Her fleet is in your hands,
    And in her fleet her Fate.

You, you, that have the ordering of her fleet,
  If you should only compass her disgrace,
When all men starve, the wild mob's million feet
  Will kick you from your place,
    But then too late, too late.

[13]
Alfred Austin
(1835–1913)

No poet laureate came more rapidly to public notice than Alfred Austin—and all thanks to his first official poem, which was published in *The Times* on 12 January 1896, only 11 days after he had taken up his appointment. With his 64 lines in praise of the Jameson Raid—a disastrous attempt, in peacetime, to overthrow Boer resistance in southern Africa—he managed not only to anger Queen Victoria and embarrass the government, but also to move Britain farther down the road to war with the Boers, which broke out three years later.

It was indeed an astonishing debut for the 60-year-old author, who had succeeded Alfred Tennyson only because of the articles he wrote in support of the Conservative party. But no less surprising was his refusal to mention the event when he came to write his exhaustive two-volume autobiography, which appeared in 1911.

Alfred Austin, who was born at Headingley, near Leeds, on 30 May 1835, came from a Roman Catholic family. His father, who was a wool merchant, sent him to Stonyhurst College in 1849. But he left when he was 17, after the headmaster had decided—for reasons apparently never revealed either to Austin or his father—that his character 'was calculated to create insubordination', and that the school would rather not have him back. So Austin moved to Oscott, another Roman Catholic college, from where in 1853 he graduated as a B.A. of London University—in those early days the university did not control the teaching of degree examinations.

In 1854 he went to the Inner Temple in London to become a barrister. But, like Shadwell and Rowe before him, he soon became disenchanted with the law (though he enjoyed debating), and on receiving a 'modest legacy' from his uncle, he decided to earn his living by writing. As he wrote in *Autobiography*, 'I now saw my way to bidding adieu to the Law, and casting my bread on the precarious water of Literature, and, most daring of all, Poetry'.

Although he had published a two-volume novel, *Five Years of It*, in 1856, his first work to attract any notice was a satirical poem called *The Season* (1861). It took a somewhat sardonic look at contemporary manners and morals, and was dedicated to the earliest of Austin's heroes, Benjamin Disraeli, then leader of the Conservative opposition in the House of Commons. Austin was particularly proud of this work, which eventually went into a third edition. More than one critic, he claimed, had called it 'the best Satire since *English Bards and Scotch Reviewers*' (Byron's attack on Wordsworth, Coleridge, and the other romantic poets). When the editor of the *Athenaeum*, an influential literary review, described it as grossly improper, Austin must have been delighted. He promptly produced a sequel, proudly called *My Satire and its Censors*.

In 1862 he issued the first draft of his long poem *The Human Tragedy* (revised versions continued to appear up to 1891). But it was so badly received he published no more verse for the next nine years. Instead, he turned again to fiction, producing a three-volume novel in 1864, and another two years later. In 1865 he found time to stand, unsuccessfully, in the Conservative interest at Taunton, Somerset, and also to marry.

The following year was a turning point in his career. Soon after getting back from 12 months' holiday in Italy, a country where he was a frequent visitor, he became a leader writer for *The Standard*, an important Conservative daily paper. Among its distinguished contributors was Lord Cranborne, who in 1896 (as Lord Salisbury) was instrumental in procuring the laureateship for Austin. Looking back on his 30 years' service, Austin wrote that he had done everything possible for the paper within the limits of his capacity: 'always, however, [he added] giving the Editor to understand that, while such was and would be my practice, I must be allowed to consider, in all I wrote, the interests of my country and the State'.

Apart from writing leaders, Austin was employed as a foreign correspondent by *The Standard*, which sent him first to Rome in 1869 to cover the Vatican Council. Before he returned home at the end of February 1870, he was assuring his readers there was no possibility the Council would agree to the proposed dogma of papal infallibility. But that is precisely what the Roman church decided, five months after Austin's departure, by which time he was preparing for his next assignment—the Franco-Prussian war, which he covered as a correspondent.

After six weeks of manoeuvring, the French army was effectively defeated on 1 September at Sedan, where Napoleon III was taken prisoner; but the war dragged on until February, when France finally surrendered and William I proclaimed himself German emperor. Early in September 1870 Austin managed to get several interviews with Bismarck, who asked him for a copy of his fiercely anti-French poem, *The Challenge Answered.* The Prussian chancellor was able to assure him that Paris would be starved into submission, and that France would be rendered harmless by the surrender of Strasbourg and Metz, conditions that the French were indeed forced to accept. Like Tennyson, then in his heyday as poet laureate, Austin was extremely pro-German and detested the French.

In 1883 Austin was invited to be one of the joint editors of the new *National Review.* This became a staunch supporter of Conservative party policy, but in its early years also published notable literary criticism by Leslie Stephen, father of Virginia Woolf and newly appointed editor of the *Dictionary of National Biography.* After four years his fellow-editor, W. J. Courthope, resigned to devote himself to literary work, leaving Austin in sole charge.

In 1885, some 15 years after Austin had published a series of articles highly critical of various contemporaries, including the laureate ('The age of Tennyson! The notion is, of course, preposterous.'), Robert Browning, Algernon Charles Swinburne, and Matthew Arnold, he was invited to meet Tennyson. From his description of this meeting (and others) Austin seems to have behaved with a good deal of false modesty, while his account manages to suggest that he upstaged the great man. 'I paused to look at a portrait of him done in his early manhood, and observed what a magnificent head of hair he must then have had. "Yes," he said, "so different from what one has now," to which I replied, quite truthfully, that he had no cause of complaint still on that score. He noticed the double semi-jocose meaning of the last phrase, and smiled; and out we passed into the open air.'

Austin was among the mourners at Tennyson's funeral in Westminster Abbey on 12 October 1892. On the coffin was a spray of bay, which Austin had acquired 11 years before on a visit to Delphi, the seat of the famous oracle of Apollo. The repercussions of the great poet's death were such that the laureateship remained vacant for three years and three months. This was a clear indication of the difficulty two successive prime ministers—Mr Gladstone and Lord Roseberry—had in selecting a successor. In the end it was a third premier, Lord Salisbury, who, after six months in office, made the decision to appoint Austin. That such a lightweight contender should have succeeded (Rudyard Kipling was only 27, William Morris refused and Gladstone found Swinburne 'absolutely impossible') shows how much importance the Conservative leader attached to Austin's long years of journalistic service to the party.

Austin's appointment was announced on 1 January 1896, when *The Times* carried its first report of the raid, on 29 December into the Transvaal by mounted forces of the British South Africa Company, led by Dr Jameson, the British Administrator of Southern Rhodesia. But after three days the invaders surrendered to the Boers, which led to the German emperor's sending a telegram of congratulation, and—a few days later—to the resignation of Cecil Rhodes, premier of Cape Colony, who had engineered the whole sorry business. Then, out of the blue, came *Jameson's Ride*, Austin's shrill poem of justification, which *The Times* published on 11 January.

Since Austin ignores the incident in his autobiography, it is difficult to know if he ever had second thoughts about the poem. In 1897, however, he was able safely to celebrate Victoria's Diamond Jubilee with a new poem. He presented it, in person, together with some roses from his garden, to his sovereign at Windsor. She accepted his gift 'with that mixture of graciousness and dignity observed by all who approached her'. In return she sent him her two books about the Highlands, suitably inscribed. After the queen died in 1901, the laureate issued *Victoria the Wise*, a collection of his writings about her; and in 1910 he was moved to mourn her son, Edward VII, when he died, in verses that recall those of his 18th-century predecessors.

During his 17 years of office Austin was subjected to as much, if not more, ridicule and abuse as any other laureate. *Punch*, in particular, found him an all-too-easy target—unfortunately, he had absolutely no sense of humour—and constantly made fun of him, his gravity, and his diminutive stature. But his self-importance made him virtually impervious to all attack.

On 2 June 1913, a few days after his 78th birthday, Austin died at Swinford Old Manor, near Ashford, Kent, which had been his home for nearly half a century and the subject of *The Garden that I Love*, his most popular work of prose.

Jameson's Ride

This Kiplingesque tribute to Dr Jameson's disastrous attempt to overthrow the Transvaal government, appeared in The Times *on 11 January 1896, ten days after Austin's appointment to the laureateship. Within days Queen Victoria had complained about it to the prime minister, Lord Salisbury, and on 18 January* Punch *published* The Laureate's First Ride, *the best of a torrent of parodies that followed swiftly:*

Say, is it song? Well—blow it!
But I'll sing it, boys, all the same
Because I'm the Laureate Poet,
That's the worst of having a name!
I must be inspired to order,
'Go, tell 'em, to save their breath!
I can rhyme to 'order' with 'border',
And jingle to 'breath' with 'death'.

Jameson, who regretted nothing, was tried in London in May 1896 under the Foreign Enlistment Act and sentenced to 15 months in prison. 'If I had succeeded,' he told the commission of enquiry, 'I should have been forgiven.'

Wrong! Is it wrong? Well, may be:
But I'm going, boys, all the same.
Do they think me a Burgher's baby,
To be scared by a scolding name?
They may argue, and prate, and order;
Go, tell them to save their breath:
Then, over the Transvaal border,
And gallop for life or death!

Let lawyers and statesmen addle
Their pates over points of law:
If sound be our sword, and saddle,
And gun-gear, who cares one straw?
When men of our own blood pray us
To ride to their kinsfolk's aid,
Not Heaven itself shall stay us
From the rescue they call a raid.

There are girls in the gold-reef city,
There are mothers and children too!
And they cry, 'Hurry up! for pity!'
So what can a brave man do?
If even we win, they'll blame us:
If we fail, they will howl and hiss.
But there's many a man lives famous
For daring a wrong like this!

So we forded and galloped forward,
As hard as our beasts could pelt,
First eastward, then trending northward,
Right over the rolling veldt;
Till we came on the Burghers lying
In a hollow with hills behind,
And their bullets came hissing, flying,
Like hail on an Arctic wind!

Right sweet is the marksman's rattle,
And sweeter the cannon's roar,
But 'tis bitterly bad to battle,
Beleagured, and one to four.
I can tell you it wasn't a trifle
To swarm over Krugersdorp glen,
As they plied us with round and rifle,
And ploughed us, again—and again.

Then we made for the gold-reef city,
Retreating, but not in rout.
They had called to us, 'Quick! for pity!'
And He said, 'They will sally out.
They will hear us and come. Who doubts it?'
But how if they don't, what then?
'Well, worry no more about it,
But fight to the death, like men.'

Not a soul had supped or slumbered
Since the Borderland stream was cleft,
But we fought, ever more outnumbered,
Till we had not a cartridge left.
We're not very soft or tender,
Or given to weep for woe,
But it breaks one to have to render
One's sword to the strongest foe.

I suppose we were wrong, were madmen,
Still I think at the Judgment Day,
When God sifts the good from the bad men,
There'll be something more to say.
We were wrong, but we aren't half sorry,
And, as one of the baffled band,
I would rather have had that foray,
Than the crushings of all the Rand.

A Voice from the West

This poem was published in The Times *on 29 March 1898, a few weeks after the battleship* Maine, *which had been sent to protect American residents during the Cuban revolt against Spain, blew up at Havana. The incident so heightened US–Spanish tension, intervention in the revolution became inevitable. The Spanish–American war, which broke out in April, forced Spain to give up Cuba and cede Puerto Rico and the Philippines to the United States. Austin obviously approved of America's imperialist ambitions, which he regarded as complementary to those of Britain.*

What is the voice I hear
  On the wind of the Western Sea?
Sentinel, listen from out Cape Clear
  And say what the voice may be.
'Tis a proud, free people calling loud to a people
    proud and free.

And it says to them, 'Kinsmen, hail!
  We severed have been too long.
Now let us have done with a worn-out tale—
  The tale of an ancient Wrong;
And our friendship last long as Love doth last,
    and be stronger than Death is strong!'

Answer them, 'Sons of the self-same race,
  And blood of the self-same clan,
Let us speak with each other face to face,
  And answer man to man;
And loyally love and trust each other as none but
    free men can.'

So fling them out to the breeze,
  Shamrock, Thistle, and Rose!
And the Star-Spangled Banner unfurl with these,
  A message to friends and foes,
Wherever the sails of peace are seen and wherever
    the war-wind blows.

A message to bond and thrall to wake:
  'For wherever we come, we twain,
The throne of the tyrant shall rock and quake,
  And his menace be void and vain;
For you are lords of a strong, young land, and
    we are lords of the main.'

Yes, this is the voice on the bluff March gale:
  'We severed have been too long.
But now we have done with a worn-out tale,
  The tale of an ancient Wrong;
And our friendship shall last long as Love doth last,
    and be stronger than Death is strong!'

Pax Britannica

Austin must have had the 'Fashoda incident' uppermost in mind when writing this poem, which appeared in The Times *on 23 November 1898. In September, British troops under Kitchener, who had just defeated the Sudanese at Omdurman and recaptured Khartoum, encountered French forces encamped at Fashoda on the upper Nile. France was planning to unite its West African possessions with those it held near the Red Sea, just as Britain hoped to establish an unbroken territorial chain from Cairo to Capetown. As British newspapers fanned the flames of anti-French feeling, war seemed imminent. But France soon backed down and retired from Fashoda. In March 1899 the two governments signed a declaration: France promised not to interfere in the Sudan; Britain agreed to allow France a free hand in Morocco. The reference to America in the penultimate verse is another reminder of Austin's vision of a UK–US axis.*

Behind her rolling ramparts England lay,
  Impregnable, and girt by cliff-built towers,
Weaving to peace and plenty, day by day,
  The long-drawn hours.

In peace Spring freed her flocks and showered her grain,
  Summer sate smiling under peaceful leaves,
And Autumn piled on the unwarlike wain
  Her sickled sheaves.

And white-winged keels flew fluttering to her shore,
  Laden with Eastern bale or Southern fleece,
And from the fields of far-off labour bore
  The spoils of Peace.

Then seeing Her within her waves so blest,
  The jealous nations, panoplied alike,
Said, 'Look, She wears no armour on her breast:
  What if we strike?'

But She, of their base greed and armed array
  Haughtily heedless, moated by her main,
Still across ocean ploughed her peaceful way
  In strong disdain.

Then each to other muttered, 'Now at last
  Her splendour shall be ours, and we shall slake
Our envy. She is pillowed on her Past,
  And will not wake.'

Slowly as stirs a lion from his bed,
  Lengthens his limbs, and crisps his mane, She rose,
Then shook out all her strength, and, flashing, said,
  'Where are my foes?'

Thus to herself She did herself reveal,
  Swiftly yet calmly put her armour on,
And, round her Empire sentinelled in steel,
  Like morning shone!

From field and forge there thronged embattled hosts,
   And that one struck the anvil, this the lyre,
And from the furnaces of war her coasts
   Were fringed with fire.

Dazed and dismayed, they veiled their futile vow;
   Some fain would be her friend, and some would nurse
Their hate till they could curb the might that now
   They could but curse.

But they who watch from where the west wind blows,
   Since great themselves, proud that their kith are great,
Said, 'See what comes when England with her foes
   Speaks at the gate!'

Then back to loom and share her people poured,
   Chanting peace-paeans as they reaped and gleaned,
While, gazing worldward, on her undrawn sword
   Watchful She leaned.

To Arms!

Austin's defiant To Arms! *is dated 23 December 1899, two months after the outbreak of the Boer war. Early that month, in what was known as 'Black Week', the British army had suffered three humiliating defeats at the hands of the Boer farmers. International hostility to Britain became intense, and complacency was shattered as people read about the army's failure to deal with the unfamiliar guerilla tactics of the enemy. To boost morale the government immediately sent out Field Marshal Lord Roberts as commander-in-chief, with Lord Kitchener as his chief of staff.*

Now let the cry, 'To Arms! To Arms!'
  Go ringing round the world;
And swift a wave-wide Empire swarms
  Round Battleflag unfurled!
Wherever glitters Britain's might,
  Or Britain's banner flies,
Leap up mailed myriads with the light
  Of manhood in their eyes;
Calling from farmstead, mart, and strand,
  'We come! And we! And we!
That British steel may hold the land,
  And British keels the sea!'

From English hamlet, Irish hill,
  Welsh hearths, and Scottish byres,
They throng to show that they are still
  Sons worthy of their sires:
That what these did, we still can do,
  That what they were, we are,
Whose fathers fought at Waterloo,
  And died at Trafalgar!
Shoulder to shoulder see them stand,
  Wherever menace be,
To guard the lordship of the land
  And the Trident of the sea.

Nor in the parent Isle alone
  Spring squadrons from the ground;
Canadian shore and Austral zone
  With kindred cry resound:
'From shimmering plain and snow-fed stream,
  Across the deep we come,
Seeing the British bayonets gleam,
  Hearing the British drum.
Foot in the stirrup, hilt in hand,
  Free men, to keep men free,
All, all will help to hold the land
  While England guards the sea!'

Comrades in arms, from every shore
   Where thundereth the main,
On to the front they press and pour
   To face the rifles' rain;
To force the foe from covert crag,
   And chase them till they fall,
Then plant for ever England's Flag
   Upon the rebel wall!
What! Wrench the Sceptre from her hand,
   And bid her bow the knee!
Not while her Yeoman guard the land,
   And her ironclads the sea!

[14]
Robert Bridges
(1844–1930)

Sixty-nine when he succeeded Alfred Austin in 1913, Robert Bridges was the oldest poet, apart from Wordsworth, to become laureate. Today his name lives on largely because in 1918 he arranged the first publication of the poems of his friend Gerard Manley Hopkins. Since then, his reputation has steadily declined—apart from a brief success in the last year of his life—while that of Hopkins has gone from strength to strength. But then, unlike Hopkins, Bridges so often bought technical excellence at the expense of emotional content, a result the Irish poet W. B. Yeats described as 'Emptiness everywhere, the whole magnificent'.

Robert Seymour Bridges was born on 23 October 1844 at Walmer, near Deal, in Kent. He was the fourth son and eighth child of a family of nine, his father John Thomas Bridges being a wealthy landowner. The boy spent his childhood at Walmer, and never forgot the serenity of the southern counties, the slow, everchanging relationship between landscape and sky. When he was nine, his father died, and the family property was sold, ensuring that he would never lack money or be forced to work for his living.

In 1854 Robert's mother, Harriett Elizabeth, married again, and the family moved to Rochdale, Lancashire, where her new husband, the Rev. Dr J. E. N. Molesworth, was vicar. That autumn Robert was sent to Eton, where he combined a love of games with a passionate concern for music and poetry. During his final year, he was joined by Digby Dolben, a distant cousin, four years his junior. Their common interest in Edward Pusey, one of the High Church leaders of the Oxford Movement, drew them close together.

In the autumn of 1863 Bridges went up to Corpus Christi, Oxford, to read classics, expecting eventually to take Holy Orders. Soon after term started, he met Gerard Manley Hopkins, also 19, who had entered Balliol College the previous April. Their friendship lasted 26 years; and during the last 12 years of Hopkin's life they corresponded regularly, each sending the other his verses for criticism. As an undergraduate, however, Bridges rapidly lost interest in religion; indeed, he left the university an agnostic.

During his final summer term (1867), Bridges stroked his college eight; and at the end of the year he took a second-class honours degree. Hopkins, who had left in June with a first, had already become a Roman Catholic. Inevitably, this altered the whole basis of their friendship; but the two were united in grief for Digby Dolben, who died suddenly that summer of heart failure. Forty-four years later, when Bridges edited Dolben's poems for publication, he provided a touching memoir of his friend. At Oxford Bridges had also become a serious student of music and an accomplished writer of melodies. Unfortunately none of his compositions survives. But in later years he compiled the *Yattendon Hymnal* (1895–99), a collection of 100 hymns chosen for the church choir at Yattendon, the Berkshire village where he lived for many years.

In 1869 Bridges became a medical student at St Bartholomew's Hospital in London. His intention was to practise medicine until he was 40, then to retire and devote himself to poetry. He took his hospital duties seriously, but still found time to write. His first volume of verse appeared in November 1873; the poems, all new, were composed in a single fortnight. Oddly enough, it was from reading a review of this book that Hopkins, by now a Jesuit novitiate, discovered that his friend actually wrote poetry. In 1874 Bridges qualified, and the following year started work as a house physician at St Bartholomew's. He managed, nevertheless, to bring out (anonymously) in 1876 the first draft of an autobiographical sonnet sequence, *The Growth of Love*, which contained 24 sonnets. By 1898, when he completed the work, the number of sonnets had increased to 69.

In 1877 Dr Molesworth died, and Bridges's mother joined him in London. By this time he had become casualty physician at the hospital. We get some idea of the work involved from a report he wrote at the end of his first year. Of the 151,000 patients admitted to hospital, he himself had seen nearly 31,000 and had prescribed

200,000 doses containing iron. In 1878 he moved to the Children's Hospital, Great Ormond Street, and later to the Great North Hospital in Holloway. But the burden of hospital work increased, until, in June 1881, he went down with pneumonia. It took him 18 months to recover, and he never returned to medicine. Instead he moved, with his mother, to Yattendon, where he now lies buried.

At Yattendon Bridges began writing poetic dramas based on the classical Athenian model. The first to be published, privately, was *Prometheus the Firegiver* (1883), written largely as a literary exercise. He completed another eight plays between 1885 and 1893; but these prove only that—like Tennyson and other Victorian poets—he never bothered to understand the practical aspects of stagecraft. In 1884 he had married Monica, eldest daughter of Alfred Waterhouse, an eminent architect, whose masterpieces include Manchester Town Hall and the Natural History Museum in London. The marriage was an extremely happy one, and the couple had a son and a daughter.

Bridges and Hopkins shared a great love for the work of John Milton, the 17th-century poet; indeed, his later blank verse contains a high degree of metrical experiment, which greatly influenced the development of their individual styles. In their different ways, too, both men realized that the use of everyday speech rhythms could make modern poetry more flexible and adventurous. But though Bridges wrote a book on the subject (*Milton's Prosody*, 1893), Hopkins issued nothing. Two years later Bridges brought out a similar study of John Keats.

During 1905 and 1906, having left Yattendon for good, Bridges spent a considerable time in Switzerland, because of his wife's poor health. In 1907 they built a house at Boar's Hill, near Oxford, where they remained for the rest of their married life. But despite the fullness of his life, the companionship of close friends, and his dedication to literature and music, Bridges remained virtually unknown. Until 1890, as his preference for private publication shows, he had no interest in personal fame. But his name was soon to become widely known. In 1912 Oxford University Press brought out a one-volume edition of his poems. Some 27,000 copies were sold within the first year.

On 2 June 1913, Alfred Austin died, and after six weeks the prime minister, Herbert Asquith, appointed Bridges poet laureate. Once again the new incumbent had to be assured he would not have to produce poems to order. Nevertheless, to commemorate his appointment—which he generously attributed to the success the university press had brought him—Bridges sent his first offering, *Noel*, to George V, just before Christmas. The king in turn passed it to *The Times*, which promptly printed it.

It was in 1913 that a group of English scholars, headed by Bridges, founded the Society for Pure English. Their aim was to preserve the purity of the language, not by 'foolish interference with living developments', but by persuading the public to accept 'certain slight modifications and advantageous changes'. Among the founders was Henry Bradley, later senior editor of *The Oxford English Dictionary*, who had become a close friend. Like Dolben and Richard Dixon (another near friend and poet), he was to be the subject of a separate memoir. The society itself had considerable influence, lasting for more than 30 years. Bridges, who also devoted much of his time to developing a phonetic alphabet, was its guiding spirit. In 1926, when the BBC Advisory Committee on Spoken English started work, he was appointed its first chairman.

In 1916 Bridges issued *The Spirit of Man*, a collection of English and French poetry and prose, designed to uplift and console his fellow countrymen in time of war. Over 50 years later the poet W. H. Auden, in a new edition of the work, said how significant it had been for his generation—it had introduced them to Hopkins.

Ever since Hopkins' death in 1889, when he had taken charge of his manuscripts, Bridges had been planning an edition of his friend's poems. But for years he hesitated, convinced people would find them 'difficult', largely because of what Hopkins called his 'sprung rhythm'. This was a revolutionary technique, derived in part from the study of Milton, in which the rhythm depends on counting stresses rather than syllables and metrical feet. Over the years, however, Bridges had gradually been inserting single poems by Hopkins into anthologies. By 1918 he decided the time had come for a definitive edition, although in fact it took O.U.P. ten years to sell out the first printing of 750 copies. In 1930 a second edition appeared, which established Hopkins as a powerful influence on contemporary poetry.

Bridges issued further collections of his own verse in 1920 and 1925. His great triumph occurred in 1930, with the publication of *The Testament of Beauty*, a philosophical poem of more than 4,000 lines. But although it went into 14 editions or impressions during its first year, it enjoys only a modest circulation today. When he died on 21 April 1930, in his 86th year, he was regarded as a major poet. Now, half a century later, attitudes have changed, and praise is reserved largely for his short lyrics. Many find it hard to identify with a writer whose education, income, and way of life separated him so decisively from his fellow men and women. But he was lucky enough to chose the life that best suited him. *Fortunatus Nimium*, his salute to life, written when he was in his seventies, shows he had no regrets:

What good have I wrought?
I laugh to have learned
That joy cannot come
Unless it be earned:

For a happier lot
Than God giveth me
It never hath been
Nor ever shall be.

Noel: Christmas Eve 1913
Pax hominibus bonae voluntatis

Bridges sent Noel, *the first poem he wrote as laureate, direct to George V. The king in turn passed it on to* The Times, *which published it on Christmas Eve 1913.*

A frosty Christmas Eve
  when the stars were shining
Fared I forth alone
  where westward falls the hill,
And from many a village
  in the water'd valley
Distant music reach'd me
  peals of bells aringing:
The constellated sounds
  ran sprinkling on earth's floor
As the dark vault above
  with stars was spangled o'er.

Then sped my thoughts to keep
  that first Christmas of all
When the shepherds watching
  by their folds ere the dawn
Heard music in the fields
  and marveling could not tell
Whether it were angels
  or the bright stars singing.

Now blessed be the tow'rs
  that crown England so fair
That stand up strong in prayer
  unto God for our souls:
Blessed be their founders
  (said I) an' our country folk
Who are ringing for Christ
  in the belfries tonight
With arms lifted to clutch
  the rattling ropes that race
Into the dark above
  and the mad romping din.

But to me heard afar
  it was starry music

Angels' song, comforting
 as the comfort of Christ
When he spake tenderly
 to his sorrowful flock:
The old words came to me
 by the riches of time
Mellow'd and transfigured
 as I stood on the hill
Heark'ning in the aspect
 of th' eternal silence.

Lord Kitchener

Lord Kitchener (b. 1850) first became famous for his reconquest of the Sudan, 1896–98. When war broke out in 1914, he became secretary of state for war, and as such his face was featured on millions of recruiting posters all over the country. He died in June 1916, when the cruiser in which he was travelling to Russia was sunk by a mine off the Orkneys.

Unflinching hero, watchful to foresee
And face thy country's peril wheresoe'er,
Directing war and peace with equal care,
Till by long toil ennobled thou wert he
Whom England call'd and bade 'Set my arm free
To obey my will and save my honour fair'—
What day the foe presumed on her despair
And she herself had trust in none but thee:

Among Herculean deeds the miracle
That mass'd the labour of ten years in one
Shall be thy monument. Thy work is done
Ere we could thank thee; and the high sea-swell
Surgeth unheeding where thy proud ship fell
By the lone Orkneys, at the set of sun.

The West Front
An English Mother, on Looking into Masefield's Old Front Line

The Old Front Line, *John Masefield's prose account of the battle of the Somme, which raged from 1 July to 13 November 1916, appeared in 1917. This offensive, which nowhere gained more than five miles, cost the British about 420,000 casualties, the French 200,000, the Germans 450,000. Adolf Hitler was among those wounded in the battle.*

No country know I so well
as this landscape of hell.
Why bring you to my pain
these shadow's effigys
Of barb'd wire, riven trees,
the corpse-strewn blasted plain?

And the names—Hebuterne
Bethune and La Bassée—
I have nothing to learn—
Contalmaison, Boisselle,
And one where night and day
my heart would pray and dwell;

A desert sanctuary,
where in holy vigil
Year-long I have held my faith
against th' imaginings
Of horror and agony
in an ordeal above

The tears of suffering
and took aid of angels:
This was the temple of God:
no mortuary of kings
Ever gathered the spoils
of such chivalry and love:

No pilgrim shrine soe'er
  hath assembled such prayer—
With rich incense-wafted
  ritual and requiem
Not beauteous batter'd Rheims
  nor lorn Jerusalem.

To the United States of America

This sonnet was written in salutation of the United States, which declared war on Germany on 6 April 1917. 'The world must be made safe for democracy,' said President Woodrow Wilson when he asked the American Congress for the declaration.

  Brothers in blood! They who this wrong began
To wreck our commonwealth, will rue the day
When first they challenged freemen to the fray,
And with the Briton dared the American.
  Now are we pledged to win the Rights of man;
Labour and justice now shall have their way,
And in a League of Peace—God grant we may—
Transform the earth, not patch up the old plan.

  Sure is our hope since he, who led your nation,
Spake for mankind; and ye arose in awe
Of that high call to work the world's salvation;
  Clearing your minds of all estranging blindness
In the vision of Beauty, and the Spirit's law,
Freedom and Honour and sweet Loving-kindness.

Our Prisoners of War in Germany

The inflated language of this poem, written in October 1918, only weeks before the Armistice, shows how deep Bridges' hatred of the enemy had become. During the war about 60,000 men from the United Kingdom were taken prisoner or posted missing.

Prisoners to a foe inhuman, Oh! but our hearts rebel:
Defenceless victims ye are, in claws of spite a prey,
Conquering your torturers, enduring night and day
Malice, year-long drawn out your noble spirits to quell.
Fearsomer than death this rack they ranged, and reckon'd well
'Twould harrow our homes, and plied, such devilish aim had they,
That England roused to rage should wrong with wrong repay,
And smirch her envied honour in deeds unspeakable.

Nor trouble we just Heaven that quick revenge be done
On Satan's chamberlains highseated in Berlin;
Their reek floats round the world on all lands 'neath the sun:
Tho' in craven Germany was no man found, not one
With spirit enough to cry Shame!—Nay, but on such sin
Follows Perdition eternal . . . and it has begun.

Der Tag: Nelson and Beatty

This poem appeared anonymously in The Times *soon after the arrival of the German High Seas Fleet (11 battleships, five battle-cruisers, eight cruisers, and 50 destroyers) off the Forth on 21 November 1918. The British Grand Fleet lay waiting in two long lines six miles apart. Admiral David Beatty, a charismatic figure, had commanded the British battle-cruisers at the battle of Jutland in 1916. ('There's something wrong with our bloody ships today', he commented after two battle-cruisers had blown up and sunk.) In June 1919 the Germans scuttled most of their ships. (The battle of Gob mentioned in verse seven refers to an encounter between the Israelites and the Philistines.)*

No doubt 'twas a truly Christian sight
When the German ships came out of the Bight,
But it can't be said it was much of a fight
   That grey November morning;
The wonderful day, the great Der Tag,
Which Prussians had vow'd with unmannerly brag
Should see Old England lower her flag
   Some grey November morning.

The spirit of Nelson, that haunts the Fleet,
Had come whereabouts the ships must meet,
But he fear'd there was some decoy or cheat
   That grey November morning,
When the enemy led by a British scout
Stole 'twixt our lines . . . and never a shout
Or a signal; and never a gun spoke out
   That grey November morning.

So he shaped his course to the Admiral's ship,
   Where Beatty stood with hand on hip
Impassive, nor ever moved his lip
   That grey November morning;
And touching his shoulder he said: 'My mate,
Am I come too soon or am I too late?
Is it friendly manoeuvres or pageant of State
   This grey November morning?'

Then Beatty said: 'As Admiral here
In the name of the King I bid you good cheer:
It's not my fault that it looks so queer
   This grey November morning.
But there come the enemy all in queues;
They can fight well enough if only they choose;
Small blame to me if the fools refuse,
   This grey November morning.

'That's Admiral Reuter, surrendering nine
Great Dreadnoughts, all first-rates of the line;
Beyond, in the haze that veils the brine
  This grey November morning,
Loom five heavy Cruisers, and light ones four,
With a tail of Destroyers, fifty or more,
Each squadron under its Commodore,
  This grey November morning.

'The least of all those captive queens
Could have knock'd your whole navy to smithereens,
And nothing said of the other machines,
  On a grey November morning,
The aeroplanes and the submarines,
Bombs, torpedoes, and Zeppelins,
Their floating mines and their smoky screens,
  Of a grey November morning.

'They'll rage like bulls sans reason or rhyme,
And next day, as if 'twere a pantomime,
They walk in like cows at milking-time,
  On a grey November morning.
We're four years sick of the pestilent mob;
—You've heard of our biblical *Battle in Gob*?—
At times it was hardly a gentleman's job
  Of a grey November morning.'

Then Nelson said: 'God bless my soul!
How things are changed in this age of coal;
For the spittle it isn't with you I'd condole
  This grey November morning.
By George! you've netted a monstrous catch:
You'll be able to pen the best dispatch
That ever an Admiral wrote under hatch
  On a grey November morning.

I like your looks and I like your name:
My heart goes out to the old fleet's fame,
And I'm pleased to find you so spry at the game
  This grey November morning.
Your ships, tho' I don't half understand
Their build, are stouter and better mann'd
Than anything I ever had in command
  Of a grey November morning.'

Then Beatty spoke: 'Sir! none of my crew,
All bravest of brave and truest of true,
Is thinking of me so much as of you
  This grey November morning.'
And Nelson replied: 'Well, thanks f' your chat.
Forgive my intrusion! I take off my hat
And make you my bow . . . we'll leave it at that,
  This grey November morning.'

[15]
John Masefield
(1878–1967)

Although ships and sailors figure prominently in the work of John Masefield, he did not—as many believe—serve before the mast as a seaman or spend years at sea. True, at the age of 16 he sailed to South America; but soon after getting there he fell ill and was sent home. The surprising thing is not how little time he spent at sea but how lasting was the effect those six months abroad had on him. What was he like, this sailor-poet, who became laureate for 37 years, a tenure of office exceeded only by Tennyson?

Masefield was born at Ledbury, Herefordshire, on 1 June 1878, the second son of Edward Masefield, a solicitor. His mother died when he was six, a few weeks after the birth of her sixth child. In 1888 John went to school in Warwick, but was removed in 1891 when his father died. That year, when he was 13, he joined H.M.S. *Conway*, a school-ship moored at Liverpool, to be trained as an officer for the merchant service. The plan had come from his aunt Kate, who with her husband, William Masefield, had taken charge of the family. Masefield left the *Conway* in March 1894 to join—as an apprentice—the *Gilcruix*, a four-masted barque bound for Iquique in Chile to pick up a cargo of nitrates. The ship took four weeks to round the notorious Cape Horn.

Back home in October, Masefield intended to leave the sea (he suffered from seasickness) and become a writer. This was easier said than done, for early the next year he was persuaded to cross the Atlantic to join a ship sailing for the Far East. However, once in New York, he changed his mind and stayed ashore. He worked in a bar for a few months, then in a carpet factory. After nearly two years he returned to England, in July 1897 and moved to London.

In 1900 he met the Irish poet, W. B. Yeats, who brought him many new friends, including the poet Laurence Binyon, who worked at the British Museum. The year 1902 marked a turning point in Masefield's career, because it saw the publication of *Salt-Water Ballads*, his first collection of verse. In the opening piece, *A Consecration*, Masefield proudly nailed his colours to the mast:

Not the ruler for me, but the ranker, the tramp of the road,
The slave with the sack on his shoulders pricked on with the goad,
The man with too weighty a burden, too weary a load.

Salt-Water Ballads was dedicated to three women, among them Constance de la Cherois Crommelin (pronounced 'Lashery Crumlin'), an Irish teacher of 35, whom Masefield had met the year before. Despite Constance's reservations about the difference in their ages—he was 24—they were married in 1902.

Ballads, a second book of poems, was published in October 1903, six months before the birth of his first child, Judith. Late in 1904 Masefield left London and joined the *Manchester Guardian*; but the night work affected his health, so he returned to London the following spring.

Masefield found himself fascinated by the discipline involved in writing for the theatre. He devised a number of lurid pieces for miniature stages that he built himself—an interest learnt from the artist Jack Yeats, W. B.'s younger brother. Masefield was soon regarded as an authority on sea matters, so he was delighted when the theatre manager Harley Granville-Barker asked his advice about the use of shanties. The contact was invaluable, for in 1907 Granville-Barker put on *The Campden Wonder*, the first play of Masefield's to be staged. A year later he produced *The Tragedy of Nan*, with his wife Lillah McCarthy in the title role. The young author, whose first novel, *Captain Margaret*, also appeared in 1908, became a close friend. Encouraged by these successes, the Masefields left London and settled in Great Hampden, Bucks.

While Constance was carrying their second child (Lewis, born July 1910), Masefield formed a close friendship with Elizabeth Robins, an American actress living in England. She was 16 years older than him, and a widow. Although the attachment lasted only until May 1910, it was peculiarly intense; Masefield called her 'Mother' (she had lost a son in infancy), no doubt because he needed that sort of emotional substitute.

The end of this relationship must have been distressing, for Masefield apparently wrote no poetry for a year. Suddenly, in 1911 came a great burst of activity. The first fruits were *The Everlasting Mercy*, a long, realistic poem about the conversion of a blasphemous, hard-drinking poacher. It made him famous almost overnight. Readers deplored the use of bad language and wondered if this were really poetry. Lord Alfred Douglas, friend of Oscar Wilde, called it 'Nine-tenths pure filth!' In 1912 came *The Widow in the Bye Street*, another poem about rural violence, followed in 1913 by *Dauber*, remarkable for its authentic description of life above and below decks.

In 1915 when the Masefields were living in Berkshire, not far from Wallingford, he went out to France for two months as a hospital orderly. Later that year he took several motorboats out to the Aegean to help the Red Cross evacuate wounded men from Gallipoli, 60 miles away. He remained there for only a matter of days before returning to England. But out of this experience came *Gallipoli* (1916), his account of the Dardanelles campaign.

Early in 1916, Sir Gilbert Parker, who was responsible for British propaganda in the United States, persuaded Masefield to spend three months over there on a paid lecture tour; and later that year he invited him to go to France to make a report on American war relief work. Towards the end of this visit, Sir Douglas Haig, the British commander-in-chief, asked him to write an account of the battle of the Somme, then raging in Flanders. In all, he spent two months in or near the battlefield; but when he returned to London in the summer of 1917, the War Office refused to let him examine the diaries of the various units involved. His book on the battle, *The Old Front Line* (1917), was confined therefore to a description of the terrain. Although a further instalment appeared in 1919 (*The Battle of the Somme*), the full history was never written.

After the war, the Masefields lived at Boar's Hill, near Oxford, moving in 1933 to the Cotswolds for six years, before finally settling at Clifton Hampden, near Dorchester, Oxfordshire. Meanwhile Masefield continued his steady output of poems, plays, and novels. These included *Reynard the Fox* (1919), perhaps his finest narrative poem, two children's classics—*The Midnight Folk* (1927) and *The Box of Delights* (1935)—and *The Bird of Dawning* (1933), a fascinating novel about the last days of sail. As a storyteller few of his contemporaries could match him.

In 1930 Robert Bridges, the poet laureate, died, and Ramsay Macdonald, the prime minister, offered Masefield the appointment. At first he hesitated, but accepted when Macdonald assured him there would be no compulsion to publish. It was a popular decision, for in a time of devastating unemployment it seemed appropriate that the laureate should be a man who supported 'the dirt and the dross, the dust and scum of the earth'.

Masefield took his duties seriously. In 1934, for instance, he helped to establish the King's Gold Medal for Poetry. But his appeals for a return to the values of an England long vanished were hardly in tune with the realities of a worldwide slump. However, he did publish verses on the launching of the *Queen Mary* (1934) and on the assassination of President Kennedy (1963). Not that he had much regard for his official utterances. When he sent a poem to *The Times*, he always included a stamped addressed envelope—just in case.

When war came in 1939, the laureate responded enthusiastically. He wrote a memorable account of the Dunkirk evacuation, *The Nine Days Wonder* (1941), following this, in 1942, with *A Generation Risen*, poems in praise of young people at war. With bitter irony, the book appeared soon after his son Lewis was killed serving with the R.A.M.C. in North Africa.

Masefield's last years were marked by sorrow and ill-health. In 1949, when he was 71, he survived both pneumonia and appendicitis; and in 1960, after 57 years of married life, Constance died, aged 93. Judith now came to live with her father; but as he entered his eighties, he had to endure cataract and increasing blindness. Masefield, however, was not a man to rest on his oars. *The Bluebells and Other Verse* was published when he was 83; *Grace before Ploughing*, short sketches about his boyhood, appeared in 1966; and finally on the eve of his 90th year, his last book of poetry, *In Glad Thanksgiving*. He died on 12 May 1967, and his ashes remain in Poet's Corner in Westminster Abbey.

534

Masefield's poem in praise of the liner Queen Mary, *known only by her job number—534—until her launching at Clydebank on 26 September 1934, appeared in the souvenir programme for the ceremony. The keel was laid in December 1930, when unemployment stood at 20 per cent, but work had ceased a year later because of the worldwide depression, and was not resumed until April 1934. This enormous undertaking—the world's first 1,000-foot liner, gross tonnage 81,000—gave work to thousands of people and soon became a powerful symbol of Britain's determination to solve its severe economic problems.*

For ages you were rock, far below light,
Crushed, without shape, earth's unregarded bone.
Then Man in all the marvel of his might
Quarried you out and burned you from the stone.

Then, being pured to essence, you were naught
But weight and hardness, body without nerve;
Then Man in all the marvel of his thought
Smithied you into form of leap and curve;

And took you, so, and bent you to his vast,
Intense great world of passionate design,
Curve after changing curving, braced and mast
To stand all tumult that can tumble brine,

And left you, this, a rampart of a ship,
Long as a street and lofty as a tower,
Ready to glide in thunder from the slip
And shear the water with majesty of power.

I long to see you leaping to the urge
Of the great engines, rolling as you go,
Parting the seas in sunder in a surge,
Shredding a trackway like a mile of snow.

With all the wester streaming from your hull
And all gear twanging shrilly as you race,
And effortless above your stern a gull
Leaning upon the blast and keeping pace.

May shipwreck and collision, fog and fire,
Rock, shoal and other evils of the sea,
Be kept from you; and may the heart's desire
Of those who speed your launching come to be.

A Prayer for the King's Majesty

Although about two million people were out of work in 1935, the year of George V's silver jubilee, Britain was beginning to emerge from the worst of the depression that had followed World War I. The king's reign had coincided with a period of unprecedented social upheaval. This poem, which Masefield read on the radio on 6 May, was the first ever broadcast by a laureate.

O God, whose mercy is our state,
Whose realms are children in Thy hand,
Who willed that, in the years of Fate,
Thy servant George should rule this land,

We thank Thee, that the years of strife
Have changed to peace, and for this thing
That Thou hast given him length of life
Under Thy hand to be our King.

O God, vouchsafe him many years
With all the world as England's friend
And England bright among her peers
With wisdom that can never end.

To Rudyard Kipling

Masefield's salute to Kipling, who died, aged 70, on 18 January 1936, could hardly have been briefer. It appeared in The Times *on 23 January, three days after the death of George V, an event that virtually ended public awareness of Kipling's departure.*

Your very heart was England's; it is just
That England's very heart should keep your dust.

On the Passing of King George V

This tribute to George V appeared in The Times *on 29 January 1936. The king, who came to the throne in 1910, had died on 20 January at the age of 71. Only eight months before, Masefield had written* A Prayer for the King's Majesty, *a poem in celebration of the monarch's silver jubilee.*

When time has sifted motives, passions, deeds
   Now complex to results and made appear
The unexpected fruits of scattered seeds,
   And scattered dust in the expected ear,
Then watchers of the life of man will know
   How spirits quickened in this ended reign,
Till what was centuries stagnant 'gan to flow
   And what was centuries fettered moved again;
How with this Ruler entered into rest
   The country's very self from slumber stirred,
Took charity as guide and hope as guest,
   And ventured to a nobler marching word.

A Prayer for the King's Reign

The wish of Edward VIII, Britain's uncrowned king, to marry Mrs Wallis Simpson, an American divorcee, led to his abdication on 10 December 1936. The new king, George VI, was a happily married family man, with two young children, Princess Elizabeth and Princess Margaret, a fact that for many represented stability in a world that seemed increasingly menacing and unpredictable. A Prayer for the King's Reign *appeared in* The Times *on 28 April 1937, two weeks before the coronation.*

O God, the Ruler over Earth and Sea,
Grant us Thy guidance in the reign to be;

Grant, that our King may make this ancient land
A realm of brothers, working mind and hand

To make the life of man a fairer thing;
God, grant this living glory to the King.

Grant, to our Queen the strength that lifts and shares
The daily burden that a monarch bears;

Grant, to them both Thy holy help to give
The hopeless, hope, the workless means to live;

The light to see, and skill to make us see,
Where ways are bad, what better ways may be;

And grace, to give to working minds the zest
To reach excelling things beyond their best;

Grant to them peace, and Thy diviner peace,
The joy of making human wars to cease;

Make wise the councils of the men who sway
The Britain here, the Britains far away;

And grant us all, that every rightness willed
In this beginning reign may be fulfilled.

On the Setting Forth of their Royal Highnesses Princess Elizabeth and the Duke of Edinburgh

Masefield's use of the word 'crown' in the last line of this short poem soon acquired a tragic, unforeseeable significance. Six days after Princess Elizabeth and the Duke of Edinburgh left Heathrow on 31 January 1952 for a tour of the Commonwealth—when The Times *published these verses—George VI died suddenly at Sandringham, and the new sovereign, Elizabeth II, had to cut short her tour and return immediately by air from Kenya.*

What can we wish you that you have not won
Already, in devotion, everywhere?
Our Southern-dwelling kindred, in their might,
Know well the arts that give a guest delight.
May all the weathers of your way be fair,
And safe returning crown your journey done.

At the Passing of a Beloved Monarch

This memorial tribute to George VI, whose reign covered nearly six years of war, appeared in The Times *on 7 February 1952, the day after the king's death.*

The everlasting Wisdom has ordained
That this rare Soul, His earthly service done
Shall leave the peoples over whom he reigned
For other service at a higher Throne,

Where Life's rewarders sing at Triumph won
In nobleness attempted and attained
Through years more terrible than any known.

What is a Nation's love? No little thing:
A vast dumb tenderness beyond all price;
Surely a power of prayer upon a wing;
The living anguish of a hope to heal
Offered by all hearts here in sacrifice
To spirits bowed in sorrow for the King
That it may touch, to comfort or anneal.

May this devotion help them in their grief.
May the devotion kindle to resolve
To make this stricken country green with leaf
Glad with another hope to be again
A Sun about which singing orbs revolve
A Kingdom grown so worthy of her Chief
That millions yet unborn shall bless her reign.

A Prayer for a Beginning Reign

Although Elizabeth II succeeded her father on 6 February 1952, her coronation did not take place until 2 June 1953. Masefield's poem appeared in The Times *on the day of the ceremony, which took place in Westminster Abbey.*

He who is Order, Beauty, Power and Glory,
He, the All-Wise, who made the eterne abyss,
The Splendour, without Presence, without Story,
Maker and Arbiter of all that is,

He set within Man's mind
All thought and image of a kingly kind;
In serving earthly Kingship we serve His.

Therefore, to Thee, All-Glorious, let us pray
For Her, Thy Destined, consecrate today.

We, then, beseech Thee, Everlasting Power,
That This, Thy dedicated Soul, may reign
In peace, in wisdom, for her mortal hour
In this beloved Land.
So guide Her with Thy ever-giving Hand
That She may re-establish standards shaken,
Set the enfettered spirit free again
With impulse green again in hearts forsaken,
With light to gladden as men reawaken
That they, after such winter-time, may flower.

Grant, King of Kings, All-Merciful, All-Knowing,
That in Her reign Her people may advance
In all fair knowledges of starry sowing
In all arts that rejoice,
In beauty of sound of instrument and voice,
In colour and form that leave the soul befriended,
In ancient joy, our Land's inheritance,
In thought, the quest for guidance never-ended
For light of Thine to make our living splendid
In service to the Queen who guides our going.

We, as a people, have been split in sunder
By all a century of thoughtless greed.
What glory in that time has been kept under?
What stunted hopes allowed?
What miles of squalid city under cloud?
Let us forget all this as done for ever;
This is a season of the springing speed
Of all a People one in an endeavour
To make our Sovereign Lady Queen indeed
Over a Kingdom worthy, the World's wonder.

John Fitzgerald Kennedy

Born in 1917, John F. Kennedy, the 35th president of the United States, was shot by a sniper on 22 November 1963, while on a visit to Dallas, Texas, and died almost immediately. He was the youngest man and the first Roman Catholic ever elected to the presidency, becoming famous for his firm handling of the Cuban missile crisis (October 1962) and for the increasing American involvement in Vietnam. The poem was printed in The Times *three days after the assassination.*

All generous hearts lament the leader killed,
The young chief with the smile, the radiant face,
The winning way that turned a wondrous race
Into sublimer pathways, leading on.

Grant to us life that though the man be gone
The promise of his spirit be fulfilled.

East Coker

T. S. Eliot, author of The Waste Land *(1922) and* Murder in the Cathedral *(1935), was born in America but came to live in England in 1914. 'Classicist in literature, royalist in politics, and Anglo-Catholic in religion'—his own description of himself—he became a British subject in 1927. His own ancestors had emigrated from East Coker, a village in Somerset, in about 1670, to settle in Massachusetts. Masefield's poem appeared in* The Times *on 8 January 1965, four days after Eliot's death.*

Here, whence his forbears sprang, a man is laid
As dust, in quiet earth, whose written word
Helped many thousands broken and dismayed
Among the ruins of triumphant wrong.
May many an English flower and little bird
(Primrose and robin redbreast unafraid)
Gladden this garden where his rest is made
And Christmas song respond, and Easter song.

[16]
Cecil Day-Lewis
(1904–1972)

By the time he was appointed poet laureate in 1968, Cecil Day-Lewis had become a pillar of the Establishment—ex-professor of poetry, Arts Council member, radio and television performer. It was a far cry from the young writer of the 1930s, who had joined the Communist party and acted as spokesman for the so-called Auden Gang of poets. But he was not the first laureate to undergo this transformation. Both Southey and Wordsworth were political idealists in their youth, but became disenchanted and had to endure considerable critical abuse.

Day-Lewis was born on 27 April 1904 at Ballintubbert, Co. Laois, in Ireland, where his father, the Rev. Frank Day Lewis, was curate. The following year the family moved to England, and when Day-Lewis was only four his mother died. Day-Lewis was looked after by one of his mother's sisters until, after 13 years, his father remarried.

In 1923, after six years at Sherborne School, Dorset, Day-Lewis won a classical exhibition to Wadham College, Oxford. Towards the end of 1925 he seems to have had his first meeting with Wystan Hugh Auden, who had just come up to Oxford and was destined in Day-Lewis's words to become 'the best poet of my generation'. Although Day-Lewis became his friend and disciple, he instinctively felt that the younger man (Auden was three years his junior) was 'perhaps best taken in small doses'.

In the summer of 1927 Day-Lewis became a master at Summer Fields, an Oxford prep school; but moved after a year to a school in Helensburgh, 20 miles from Glasgow. At the end of 1928 he married Constance Mary King, daughter of a master at Sherborne, where the pair had first met. He brought out his first noteworthy book of verse—*Transitional Poem*—a sequence of lyrics dealing with his development from adolescent to adult in 1929. The unusual blend of classical reference and technological image made it seem to many a poetical breakthrough.

In 1930 Day-Lewis took a new teaching post at Cheltenham. Later that year, when Mary was pregnant, he began work on another sequence of poems, *From Feathers to Iron*. This described his own experiences as a father during the gestation and birth of his first child, Sean, who was born in August 1931, the month before the new work appeared. One influential reviewer decided it was an important landmark, as significant as Walt Whitman's *Leaves of Grass* (1855) or T. S. Eliot's *The Waste Land* (1922). But the real literary landmark of the 1930s, appeared the following year. This was *New Signatures*, a collection of pieces by new poets, including Day-Lewis, Auden, Stephen Spender, and William Empson.

Day-Lewis's contribution to *New Signatures* consisted of three pieces from *The Magnetic Mountain*, his next sequence of poems, which was dedicated to Auden and appeared in 1933. Outspoken in its condemnation of capitalism, it was surprisingly vague about the sort of society required to replace it, although it had interesting things to say about the need for strong leaders. Appropriately enough, it was published in the spring of 1933, soon after Hitler became Chancellor of Germany.

In 1935, the year after his second son, Nicholas, was born, Day-Lewis completed *A Question of Proof*, the first of his 20 detective novels, all produced under the pseudonym of Nicholas Blake. Written to raise money for roof repairs, it featured his sleuth Nigel Strangeways, a character originally based on Auden. Success in this field led to an approach from another publisher, for whom he agreed to write three novels in three years for an advance of £300 a year. He abandoned teaching and took up full-time writing. That same year he also brought out a book of collected poems and a new work, *A Time to Dance*.

By 1936 Day-Lewis had joined the Communist party and published a morality play, *Noah and the Waters*. The play, which was never performed, reflected his inability to choose between the status quo and the forces of revolution. But for all its political dedication, the play impressed no one, not even the *Daily Worker*, the party newspaper. Geoffrey Grigson, then editor of *New Verse*, a magazine founded in 1932, called it 'fake poetry and fake Auden'.

In many ways, 1936 was the pivotal point of the thirties. It was the year Germany reoccupied the Rhineland, the year Italy took possession of Abyssinia; above all, it marked the start of the Spanish Civil War, an event that made world war seem inevitable. Day-Lewis remained an active party worker for about two years; but his commitment began to wane as he found himself forced to choose between politics and poetry. Personal involvements must also have played their part: after buying a house at Musbury, over the Devon border from Lyme Regis, he fell in love with a neighbour's wife. The passionate affair culminated in the birth of a child, which must have been devastating for Mary.

During 1940 Day-Lewis devoted much of his time to the local Home Guard and to his translation of the *Georgics*, Virgil's poem about agriculture and stock-breeding, which appeared that autumn. Before the outbreak of war, he had applied for a job with the proposed Ministry of Information, but was not called to London until March 1941. He remained with the ministry for five years. Emotional complications, however, continued, for during his first year in London, he fell in love with the novelist Rosamond Lehmann. Yet despite this commitment and the demands imposed by his family and his job, he still found time to help set up the Apollo Society, a group of actors, poets and musicians, which toured the country giving readings and recitals.

In 1943, *Word Over All*, a collection of 31 poems, was published, and sold well. Soon after the war ended Day-Lewis was asked to give the Clark Lectures at Cambridge. Delivered early in 1946, they proved a great success and were later published under their original title, *The Poetic Image*. That autumn, having now left his government job, he joined the publishers Chatto and Windus, as their senior reader. He remained with them until the end of his life, becoming a director after eight years.

In 1948 he produced *The Otterbury Incident*, his second adventure novel for boys, which has sold about 250,000 copies, making it far and away the most successful of all his works. But for Day-Lewis the most important event of 1948 was his meeting with the 23-year-old actress Jill Balcon, daughter of Sir Michael Balcon, the film producer. By 1949 they were in love, a shattering discovery for his wife and for Rosamond Lehmann, to say nothing of the mother of his illegitimate child. The situation was not resolved until 1950, when Mary agreed to divorce him, and he was able to remarry in April 1951. Two children were born of this second marriage. Earlier that year he had been elected professor of poetry at Oxford, an appointment that involved little more than his giving three lectures a year for five years. He also completed his translation of Virgil's *Aeneid* in time for it to be broadcast as part of the Festival of Britain celebrations.

As the years passed, Day-Lewis became an increasingly well-known public figure. In 1957 he joined the group of advisers who recommend awards for the Queen's Gold Medal for Poetry (an honour established in 1934). Four years later he was appointed chairman of the Poetry Panel of the Arts Council, and in 1964 he himself became a Companion of Literature. During the winter of 1964–65, he spent six months at Harvard University, giving a series of lectures on the English lyric, which were published as *The Lyric Impulse* (1965). In 1965 he took over as first chairman of the Literature Panel of the Arts Council.

When Masefield died in May 1967, Day-Lewis was one of the favourite candidates to succeed him, although it was nearly seven months before the prime minister, Harold Wilson, approached him. The appointment on 2 January 1968 made front-page news. As laureate he now presided over the committee responsible for choosing the winner of the Queen's Medal, which gave him a further opportunity to enlist support for the arts.

In the last few years of his life, Day-Lewis showed great courage, for he had to contend not only with dire ill-health but also with his growing conviction that he had written nothing of real value. In April 1971, he was found to have cancer. Somehow, in the first months of 1972, he summoned enough strength to make a series of poetry programmes for television, before he died on 22 May 1972 at Hadley Common in north London. He was buried at Stinsford, Dorset, close by the heart of Thomas Hardy, the poet who had been perhaps the greatest influence on his work.

Then and Now

This poem, Day-Lewis's first official laureate piece, was commissioned by the Daily Mail *as a contribution to the 'I'm Backing Britain' campaign, and was published on the front page of the paper on 5 January 1968. The campaign was based on a new-year resolution put forward by five women typists at a factory in Surbiton, Surrey, who suggested that everyone should work an extra 30 minutes a day without pay. The Duke of Edinburgh said it was the most heartening news he'd heard in 1967. But the trade unions, worried by rising unemployment—600,000 people were then out of work—were lukewarm in their response. By the end of the year the issue was dead and forgotten.*

Do you remember those mornings after the blitzes
When the living picked themselves up and went on living—
Living, not on the past, but with an exhilaration
Of purpose, a new neighbourliness of danger?

Such days are here again. Not the bansheeing
Of sirens and the beat of terrible wings
Approaching under a glassy moon. Your enemies
Are nearer home yet, nibbling at Britain's nerve.

Be as you were then, tough and gentle islanders—
Steel in the fibre, charity in the veins—
When few stood on their dignity or lines of demarcation,
And few sat back in the padded cells of profit.

Boiler-room, board-room, backroom boys, we all
Joined hearts to make a life-line through the storm.
No haggling about overtime when the heavy-rescue squads
Dug for dear life under the smouldering ruins.

The young cannot remember this. But they
Are graced with that old selflessness. They see
What's needed; they strip off dismay and dickering,
Eager to rescue our dear life's buried promise.

To work then, islanders, as men and women
Members one of another, looking beyond
Mean rules and rivalries towards the dream you could
Make real, of glory, common wealth, and home.

Hail Teesside!

The county borough of Teesside came into being on 1 April 1968 at Middlesbrough, when its charter was presented by Lord Normanby, Lord Lieutenant of the North Riding. The six towns that united to form the new administrative unit were Middlesbrough, Stockton, Redcar, Thornaby, Eston, and Billingham. The Evening Gazette*, which is based in Middlesbrough, commissioned the poem and printed it on its front page on the day of amalgamation.*

Old ironmasters and their iron men
With northern fire, grit, enterprise began it
A hundred years ago. Later, we scan it—
Desolate homesteads welded into one,
Hamlets grown up to towns, deep anchorages
Gouged out of sand, wastes blossoming with the fierce
White rose of foundries. So the pioneers
Printed their work on nature's open page.
Their steel made bridges from Sydney to Menai;
Their ships networked the sea. Gain was in view
But inch by inch out of the gain there grew
A greater thing—sense of community.

Bridges are for drawing men together
By closing gaps. Could those rough ghosts return,
They'd find a world of difference, but discern
That here is the same breed of men and weather.
You are bridge-builders still. Only, today
You draw six towns into a visioned O,
Spanning from town to town the ebb and flow
Of destiny. A dream is realised. May
The northern kindliness and northern pride
See, as your forebears would, the future in it.
Here, a new span—our lives shall underpin it
And earn fresh honours for our own Teesside.

For the Investiture

The investiture of Prince Charles as prince of Wales at Caernarvon Castle on 1 July 1969 was something of a television spectacular, watched by a worldwide audience of 500 million people. The laureate's poem was printed in The Guardian, *together with a Welsh translation provided by E. Gwyndaf Evans, the Archdruid of Wales.*

Today bells ring, bands play, flags are unfurled,
  Anxieties and feuds lie buried
Under a ceremonial joy. You, sir, inherit
  A weight of history in a changing world,
Its treasured wisdom and its true
  Aspirings the best birthday gift for you.

Coming of age, you come into a land
  Of mountain, pasture, cwm, pithead,
Steelworks. A proud and fiery people, thoroughbred
  For singing, eloquence, rugby football, stand
Beneath Caernarvon's battlements
  To greet and take the measure of their prince.

But can they measure his hard task—to be
  Both man and symbol? With the man's
Selfhood the symbol grows in clearer light, or wanes.
  Your mother's grace, your father's gallantry
Go with you now to nerve and cheer you
  Upon the crowded, lonely way before you.

May your integrity silence each tongue
  That sneers or flatters. May this hour
Reach through its pageantry to the deep reservoir
  Whence Britain's heart draws all that is fresh and young.
Over the tuneful land prevails
  One song, one prayer—God bless the Prince of Wales.

Battle of Britain

This poem was commissioned for the souvenir programme issued at the première *of the* Battle of Britain *film, which opened in London on 15 September 1969. At the time of the battle, the author himself was living in Devon, where he was a member of the Home Guard. Among those who attended the film* première *was Air Chief Marshal Lord Dowding, head of R.A.F. Fighter Command during 1940.*

What did we earth-bound make of it? A tangle
Of vapour trails, a vertiginously high
Swarming of midges, at most a fiery angel
Hurled out of heaven, was all we could descry.

How could we know the agony and pride
That scrawled those fading signatures up there,
And the cool expertise of those who died
Or lived through that delirium of the air?

Grounded on history now, we re-enact
Such lives, such deaths. Time, laughing out of court
The newspaper heroics and the faked
Statistics, leaves us only to record.

What was, what might have been: fighter and bomber,
The tilting sky, tense moves and counterings;
Those who outlived that legendary summer;
Those who went down, its sunlight on their wings.

And you, unborn then, what will you make of it—
This shadow-play of battles long ago?
Be sure of this: they pushed to the uttermost limit
Their luck, skill, nerve. And they were young like you.

[17]
John Betjeman
(1906–   )

No poet since Tennyson has become such a national figure as Sir John Betjeman, the present laureate, and in his own lifetime he has earned affection and fame on a scale equalled only by that great predecessor. By the time he took office in 1972, more than 200,000 copies of his *Collected Poems* had been sold; and his own performances on radio and on television had made him a household name—a writer whose passionate convictions about architecture and the countryside endeared him to millions of people.

John Betjeman is an only child, born in Highgate, North London, on 28 August 1906. His father, Ernest Betjeman, descended from a Dutchman who settled in London early in the 19th century, was a designer and manufacturer of *objets d'art*—expensive dressing cases, furniture, silverware, and the like. From the time Betjeman was born, it was his father's wish that he would eventually take over the family business. But as soon as he could read and write, the boy made up his mind to be a poet. He wished to know nothing about the business, a decision that made him feel intensely guilty and soon clouded relations with his father, who was, unfortunately, stone-deaf.

After kindergarten, Betjeman was sent to Highgate Junior School. When he was about ten, he handed some of his verse to 'the American master', who was rumoured to like poetry. This was none other than T. S. Eliot, who had settled in England in 1914 at the age of 26, but had not yet produced his first book. Apparently, Eliot made no comment whatsoever; and when Betjeman met him in later life he did not refer to the incident.

From Highgate Betjeman went to the Dragon (preparatory) School at Oxford, and thence to Marlborough College, in Wiltshire. He hated the compulsory games and the lack of privacy, and lived in dread of beatings and debaggings. After five years he went up to Magdalen College, Oxford, to read English, and became a pupil of C. S. Lewis, later famous as the author of *The Allegory of Love*, *The Screwtape Letters*, and a number of children's books. Lewis was only eight years older than his pupil, but the two did not get on well; Betjeman was too intoxicated with his newfound freedom from restrictions to do any academic work or attend regular tutorials. He described himself later as having been 'trivial, baroque, incense-loving; a diner with a great admiration for the landowning classes and the houses and parks in which they were lucky enough to live'.

The final chapter of his autobiographical poem, *Summoned by Bells* (1960), recalls those years at Oxford, when his friends and contemporaries included Evelyn Waugh, Osbert Lancaster, and W. H. Auden. But despite Betjeman's love of smart friends, fast cars, lavender-scented baths, and country house visiting, it's clear that he is painting a very one-sided picture of his undergraduate life. One of his early admirers, the classical scholar Maurice Bowra (like Lewis, only eight years his senior), was then Dean of Wadham College. He, said Betjeman, 'taught me far more than all my tutors did', and introduced him to the poetry of Thomas Hardy, whose work was to have such a great influence on him.

While he was at the Dragon School, Betjeman had already begun to explore the Oxford colleges and churches, accompanied by a fellow pupil, and these voyages of discovery continued during the holidays when he returned to Chelsea where his family now lived. Together the two boys, who were near neighbours, travelled the length and breadth of the Underground network, and got to know all the different railway systems in London. On his own, Betjeman would browse for hours in bookshops, and on Sundays, obsessed with an immense longing for the past, he would wander in the City, letting its silent spaces work their magic on him.

At Marlborough, he was able to explore the surrounding Wiltshire countryside, and learned to sketch and paint. Above all other experiences, however, he valued what he called the ecstasy of writing poetry. And during the holidays there were the continuing joys of Cornwall and its empty beaches, where he had spent summer holidays ever since he was a small boy.

No wonder Bowra, in his *Memories 1898–1939* (1966) said that Betjeman 'was already a learned man when he came to Oxford, and there he greatly extended his learning'. Before reaching university he had discovered the supreme interests of his life, all those things that now seem so inevitably part of his personality; and at Oxford he became a devout High Churchman, and found his distinctive note, writing poems that are instantly recognizable as his.

Betjeman left Oxford without taking a degree. Of all things, he failed a divinity exam, which had to be passed before he could enter for his final exams. His father stopped his allowance, so he had to take whatever work he could find. He began as a prep-school master, teaching maths, French, games, and divinity, and then he tried his hand at journalism. He worked for a time on the *Architectural Review*, and then on the *Evening Standard*. Here he did film criticism and helped with the Londoner's Diary (at that time, contributors to this famous feature included Randolph Churchill, Malcolm Muggeridge, and the novelist Howard Spring).

In 1932 he published *Mount Zion: or, In Touch with the Infinite*, his first book of poetry, which included such now-famous poems as *Death in Leamington*, *Hymn*, and *Croydon*. The following year he married Penelope Chetwode, whose father was then commander-in-chief of the Indian army. They have a son and a daughter. That same year Betjeman produced *Ghastly Good Taste; or, A Depressing Story of the Rise and Fall of English Architecture*, the first of several books dealing with architecture and topography. He followed this in 1937 with his second book of poetry, *Continual Dew: A Little Book of Bourgeois Verse*, which included the poems entitled *Dorset*, *Slough*, and *Death of King George V*. By now the Betjemans were living at Uffington in Berkshire, remaining there until 1941, when he became UK press attaché in Dublin. In 1943 he was back in England, working at the Admiralty before spending two years with the British Council (1944–46).

After the war Betjeman began to make a new name for himself on radio and television. He received the Heinemann Award in 1949 for his *Selected Poems* (published the previous year), and produced a number of county guides. In 1958 his *Collected Poems* established him as an immediate bestseller. One hundred thousand copies were sold in the first six months. (Another of his most popular works, a guide to English parish churches, came out the same year.) Today, more than 20 years later, sales of the *Collected Poems* are approaching half a million. *Summoned by Bells*, which was published in 1960, the year he won the Queen's Gold Medal for Poetry, has also enjoyed great popularity, having now sold more than 100,000 copies. He was knighted in 1969.

When Day-Lewis died on 22 May 1972, Betjeman was—in terms of his immense popularity, alone—a very strong contender for the laureateship, although he himself thought Philip Larkin (born 1922) author of *The Less Deceived* and *The Whitsun Weddings*, stood the best chance. But, in the event, Betjeman was appointed to the post on 10 October 1972. Interviewed by *The Times*, he said how pleased he was to succeed his friend Day-Lewis, and added: 'I am pleased also to be the successor of Tennyson, Wordsworth and Bridges but not quite so pleased to be the successor of Alfred Austin. I am sure he wrote some good poetry. I have been reading his work looking for it.' Characteristically, he went on to say that he had regarded himself as a failure all his life, a feeling reinforced by his frequent sackings as a journalist. His appointment as laureate could not alter that view: 'I don't think I am any good; and if I thought I was any good, I wouldn't be any good.' One wonders what Dryden, the first of his predecessors, would have made of that.

Day-Lewis, like all laureates since 1790, had been receiving £27 instead of the traditional butt of wine. But when Betjeman took over he was persuaded by the Privy Purse Office to renounce the money and take the equivalent in wine. Not that a grateful monarch wanted to go back to the 126 gallons after all these years. That would indeed have been a munificent gesture. What he actually gets—apart from the £70 from the civil list—is just £27 worth of wine from the Queen's wine merchant.

Since his appointment, Betjeman has written only three poems in official recognition of specific state occasions. He has celebrated the wedding of Princess Anne (1973), the Queen's silver jubilee (1977), and the Queen Mother's 80th birthday. None of these pieces has been very successful. Indeed, the reaction of the Press has been almost uniformly hostile. But if Sir John knows the history of the other laureates—and we can be sure he does—he cannot have been surprised.

14 November 1973

'I wanted it to be quite clear, very simple, and not like a Christmas card,' said Sir John Betjeman, referring to this poem, his first official piece as laureate. It was written to celebrate the wedding of Princess Anne to Capt. Mark Phillips on 14 November 1973. The ceremony took place at Westminster Abbey.

Hundreds of birds in the air
   And millions of leaves on the pavement,
And Westminster bells ringing on
   To palace and people outside—
And all for the words 'I will'
   To love's most willing enslavement.
All of our people rejoice
   With venturous bridegroom and bride.

Trumpets blare at the entrance,
   Multitudes crane and sway.
Glow, white lily in London,
   You are high in our hearts today!

Jubilee Hymn

Betjeman's hymn for the silver jubilee of Queen Elizabeth was first performed at the Albert Hall in London on 6 February 1977. Music was by Malcolm Williamson, Master of the Queen's Music. Unfavourable com-

ment in newspapers provoked the author into remarking, 'The words were meant for singing, not reading, and have therefore plentiful long vowels. "God Save the Queen" is not poetry, but it sings well. This was written to sing well.'

In days of disillusion,
However low we've been
To fire us and inspire us
God gave to us our Queen.

She acceded, young and dutiful,
To a much-loved father's throne;
Serene and kind and beautiful,
She holds us as her own.

And twenty-five years later
So sure her reign has been
That our great events are greater
For the presence of our Queen.

Hers the grace the Church has prayed for,
Ours the joy that she is here.
Let the bells do what they're made for!
Ring our thanks both loud and clear.

From that look of dedication
In those eyes profoundly blue
We know her coronation
As a sacrament and true.

Chorus

For our Monarch and her people,
United yet and free,
Let the bells from ev'ry steeple
Ring out loud the jubilee.

For the Queen Mother

This poem for the Queen Mother was written to celebrate her 80th birthday on 4 August 1980. As Elizabeth Bowes-Lyon, daughter of the 14th earl of Strathmore, she married Prince Albert, duke of York (later George VI) in 1923.

We are your people;
Millions of us greet you
On this your birthday
Mother of our Queen.
Waves of goodwill go
Racing out to meet you,
You who in peace and war
Our Faithful friend have been.
You who have known the sadness of bereavement,
The joyfulness of family jokes
And times when trust is tried.
Great was the day for our United Kingdoms
And God Bless the Duke of York
Who chose you as his bride.

Sir John Betjeman's poem in celebration of the wedding on 29 July 1981 of Charles, Prince of Wales, to Lady Diana Spencer appears opposite the title page.

Index

Addison, Joseph (1672–1719) 55, 56
Albert, Prince (1819–61) 6, 7, 127, 128–32, 135, 136
Anne, Princess (1950–) 196, 197
Anne, Queen (1665–1714) 3, 34, 38–40, 41, 46, 56, 67
Arts Council of Great Britain 184, 187
Aubrey, John (1626–1797) 2, 21
Auden, W. H. (1907–73) 162, 184, 185, 186, 194
Austin, Alfred 7, 67, 105, **148–60,** 159, 162, 196. Selection 150–57

Balcon, Jill (1925–) 187
BBC Advisory Committee on Spoken English 162
Betjeman, Sir John 8, 90, **196–202.** Selection 197–99
Binyon, Laurence (1869–1943) 7, 172
Bowra, Sir Maurice (1898–1971) 194, 195
Bridges, Robert 7, **161–73,** 175, 196. Selection 163–71
Byron, Lord (1788–1824) 116, 147

Cambridge 6, 10, 20, 55, 56, 58, 77, 78, 127, 133, 186
Charles, prince of Wales (1948–) 190
Charles I (1600–49) 1, 9
Charles II (1630–85) 1, 2, 9, 10, 11, 13, 22, 43
Charlotte Augusta, princess of Wales (1796–1817) 117–21, 128
Charlotte, Queen (1744–1818) 122–23
Chaucer, Geoffrey (1340?–1400) 13, 93
Cibber, Colley 3, 4, 55, **66–76,** 77, 79. Selection 70–76
Cibber, Theophilus (1703–57) 57
Coleridge, Samuel Taylor (1772–1834) 113, 114, 126, 147
Congreve, William (1670–1729) 55
Cowley, Abraham (1618–67) 13, 33

Daily Mail 188
Daily Worker 185
Davenant, Sir William (1606–68) 1, 2, 9, 21, 32, 44
Day-Lewis, Cecil 8, 66, **184–92,** 196. Selection 188–92
Dryden, John 1, 2, 3, **9–20,** 20, 21, 23, 24, 31, 32, 45, 47, 55, 56, 58, 196 Selection 13–20
Dublin 31, 195
Duck, Stephen (1705–56) 4, 68

Edinburgh, duke of (1921–) 180, 188
Edward VII (1841–1910) 142, 150
Edward VIII (1894–1972) 179
Eliot, T. S. (1888–1965) 9, 183, 185, 193
Elizabeth II (1926–) 180, 181, 196, 197
Elizabeth (Queen Mother) (1900–) 196, 199
Eusden, Laurence (1688–1730) 3, **55–65,** 68, 113. Selection 59–65
Evening Gazette 189
Evening Standard 195

Fitzgerald, Edward (1809–83) 135
French Revolution 102, 105, 107, 113, 114, 124, 125

Garrick, David (1717–79) 44, 69, 78, 80
Garth, Sir Samuel (1661–1719) 56
Gay, John (1685–1732) 56, 68
Gentleman's Magazine 4, 69
George I (1660–1727) 34, 35, 41, 46, 47, 51, 53, 56, 57, 59, 67, 68, 79
George II (1683–1760) 58, 80
George III (1738–1820) 3, 5, 78, 81, 83, 93, 95, 98, 102, 103, 104, 107, 115, 116, 122
George IV (1762–1830) 6, 101, 117
George V (1865–1936) 162, 163, 177, 178
George VI (1895–1952) 179, 180, 199
Gladstone, William (1809–98) 133, 136, 144, 145, 149
Gold Medal for Poetry 7, 175, 187, 196
Goldsmith, Oliver (1730–74) 68, 80

Gray, Thomas (1716–71) 4, 55, 77, 79
Guardian, The (ex-*Manchester Guardian*) 173, 190

Hardy, Thomas (1840–1928) 7, 187, 194
Hopkins, Gerard Manley (1844–89) 159, 160, 161, 162, 163
Housman, A. E. (1859–1936) 7
Hunt, Leigh (1784–1859) 6

James II (1633–1701) 2, 12, 22, 24, 26, 35, 38, 57
Jameson, Dr Leander Starr (1853–1917) 7, 149, 150
Johnson, Dr Samuel (1709–84) 11, 32, 46, 91, 92, 102
Jonson, Ben (1572–1637) 1, 2, 21, 33, 101

Keats, John (1795–1821) 161
Kipling, Rudyard (1865–1936) 7, 149, 178

Larkin, Philip (1922–) 196
Lewis, C. S. (1898–1963) 197
London 10, 31, 34, 46, 57, 58, 78, 80, 92, 146, 160, 161, 172, 173, 186, 193, 194
London Gazette 5
Lord Chamberlain 3, 5

Mary II (1662–94) 25
Masefield, John 7, 66, 77, 166, **176–84,** 187. Selection 176–83
Mason, William (1724–97) 4, 79, 80, 90
Massinger, Philip (1583–1640) 43
Master of King's/Queen's Music 3, 70, 197
Milton, John (1608–74) 89, 92, 161, 162
Monmouth, duke of (1649–85) 2, 11, 13, 22, 23
Morris, William (1834–96) 7, 149

National Book League 7
New Signatures 185
New Verse 186

Oxford 4, 77, 89, 90, 91, 93, 101, 113, 159, 160, 184, 187, 194

Pepys, Samuel (1633–1703) 21
Pope, Alexander (1688–1744) 4, 23, 48, 58, 68, 69, 77, 89, 91
Prince Regent 5, 115, 117, 128. *See also* George IV
Punch 150
Pye, Henry James 5, **101–12,** 113, 115. Selection 105–12

Quarterly Review 114, 116
Quillinan, Edward (1791–1851) 6, 127, 128

Rogers, Samuel (1763–1855) 6, 7, 135
Rowe, Nicholas 3, **43–54,** 57, 67, 104, 146. Selection 47–54

Scott, Walker (1771–1832) 5, 104, 115
St James's Palace 3, 70
Shadwell, Thomas 3, 11, 12, **20–30,** 31, 32, 33, 146. Selection 24–30
Shakespeare, William (1564–1616) 21, 31, 32, 43, 45, 46, 67, 69, 103, 104, 113, 137
Shelley, Percy Bysshe (1792–1822) 116
Southey, Robert 5, 6, 77, 101, 109, **113–24,** 124, 126, 127, 185. Selection 117–23
Spectator, The 55, 56
Spenser, Edmund (1552–99) 89, 90, 93
Swinburne, Algernon Charles (1837–1909) 7, 9, 149

Tate, Nahum 3, 11, 23, **31–42,** 46, 67. Selection 35–42
Tennyson, Alfred 6, 7, 77, **135–47,** 148, 161, 172, 193, 196
Times, The 6, 115, 136, 137, 142, 143, 144, 146, 149, 150, 154, 162, 163, 168, 175, 178, 179, 180, 181, 183, 196,
Tonson, Jacob (1656?–1736) 56

Victoria, Queen (1819–1901) 6, 117, 127, 128, 135, 136, 142, 146, 149, 150

Warton, Joseph (1722–1800) 89, 92
Warton, Thomas 4, 5, **89–101,** 102. Selection 93–100
Whitehead, William 4, **77–88,** 92. Selection 81–88
William III (1650–1702) 2, 12, 23, 24, 26, 34, 35, 44, 55, 57, 59, 66
William IV (1756–1837) 128
Wordsworth, William 6, 7, 114, 116, **124–32,** 135, 147, 159, 184, 196. Selection 128–32

Yeats, W. B. (1865–1939) 159, 172